MathConnex

User's Guide

MathSoft, Inc.
101 Main Street
Cambridge
Massachusetts 02142
USA
http://www.mathsoft.com/

MathSoft
$\Sigma + \sqrt{\ } - = \times \int \div \delta$

Mathcad, *Axum*, and *S-PLUS* are registered trademarks of MathSoft, Inc. *Electronic Book, QuickSheets, MathConnex, ConnexScript, Collaboratory, IntelliMath, Live Symbolics,* and the MathSoft logo are trademarks of MathSoft, Inc.

Microsoft, Windows, IntelliMouse, and the Windows logo are registered trademarks of Microsoft Corp. *Windows NT* is a trademark of Microsoft Corp.

OpenGL is a registered trademark of Silicon Graphics, Inc.

MATLAB is a registered trademark of The MathWorks, Inc.

Other brand and product names referred to are trademarks or registered trademarks of their respective owners.

Printed in the United States of America. First printing: August 1998.

Table of Contents

1: About MathConnex   **1**
What is MathConnex?   2
Using MathConnex   3
Additional sources of information   4

2: The MathConnex Workspace   **5**
Starting MathConnex   6
Menus, Toolbar, and Status Bar   7
Component palettes   10
The Worksheet   11
The MathConnex Explorer   16

3: Creating and Running a System   **19**
Overview   20
Placing components on the Worksheet   21
Getting organized   23
Configuring the components   26
Wiring components together   30
Running and stopping a system   31
Changing the appearance of components   35

4: Components   **39**
Overview   40
Components for generating, importing, and exporting data   43
Components for viewing results   49
Computational components   61
Components for controlling data flow   72
Other components   77

5: Advanced Topics   **81**
MathConnex run model   82
Scripted Object component   84
Using ConnexScript   88

Index   **99**

Chapter 1
About MathConnex

Welcome to MathConnex! This chapter provides a brief overview of MathConnex and how you use it with other computational programs and data sources.

What is MathConnex?

Basic features and operation.

Using MathConnex

Suggested uses with Mathcad, S-PLUS, and other applications or data sources.

Additional sources of information

Where to get help on MathConnex if you need it.

What is MathConnex?

MathConnex is an environment for visually integrating and linking applications and data sources to create heterogeneous computational systems. By providing visual components for each data source or application in a system—such as a Mathcad component, an Axum component, an S-PLUS Graph component, an S-PLUS Script component, an Excel component, and a File Read/Write component—MathConnex lets you manage the flow of data from one application or data source to another.

You can easily create a system consisting of Mathcad worksheets, S-PLUS scripts, objects from other applications, and data sources by:

■ Dragging components from the Component Palettes and dropping them into the MathConnex Worksheet.

■ Wiring the components together to indicate data flow.

■ Using Toolbar controls to run the system.

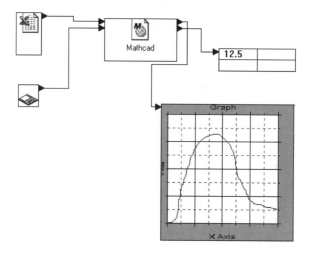

You can think of each visual component in the system as a separate object or process, receiving input, calculating, and producing output. MathConnex seamlessly handles all the data passing and process execution, allowing you to focus on the system as a whole.

MathConnex features

MathConnex makes it easy for you to design, activate, and publish systems of applications and data sources by allowing you to:

■ Access 20 visual components for importing and exporting data, for performing calculations and viewing results, and for controlling the flow of data from one component to the next.

■ Drag and drop components into the Worksheet.

- Capture a group of connected components as a module to use in other projects.

- Integrate and manage data and computations between different applications.

- Perform mathematical calculations using Mathcad, S-PLUS, Axum, Excel, and MATLAB.

- Analyze and debug calculations.

- Compute using the ConnexScript math programming language.

- Script embedded OLE components using VBScript or JScript.

- Work productively in a truly customizable and extensible environment.

Using MathConnex

Given the variety of components available for integration into a system, you can use MathConnex to design an endless number of different systems involving different applications and data sources. For example, you can use MathConnex to:

- Integrate Mathcad or S-PLUS calculations with those from applications such as Excel and MATLAB.

- Link an Excel data component with an S-PLUS Script component that calculates a a statistical simulation, then wire the output to an S-PLUS Graph component to display the results as an S-PLUS scatter plot.

- Chain worksheets together and pass data from one to the next, or loop through a worksheet by passing the output from a worksheet back into itself as input.

- Facilitate the development of a large project: break it up into subsections, design each as a MathConnex module, and assemble the subsections into a MathConnex project, using conditionals to control the flow of data from one module to another.

A note about other applications

The built-in components in MathConnex include several designed especially to work with other computational programs: MathSoft's Mathcad, S-PLUS, and Axum, Microsoft Excel, and MATLAB from The MathWorks. To use the computational components, you'll need to have installed an appropriate version of the corresponding application on your system: Mathcad 8 or higher, S-PLUS 4.5 or higher, Axum 5.0c or higher, Excel for Windows 95 or higher, or MATLAB 4.2c or higher. See the Release Notes accompanying your MathConnex installation media for current compatibility information.

A note about performance and memory

To run MathConnex, you should have at least 16 megabytes of memory installed on your computer. Be aware that many MathConnex components are specialized OLE objects that allow you to connect to an application or data source. Using these components therefore requires additional memory, as well as additional processing power, to run the applications with which they are associated. To use the Mathcad and Excel components together in MathConnex, for example, we recommend that you have at least 32 megabytes of memory installed on your system.

Additional sources of information

This guide is designed to provide you with enough information so that you can immediately begin creating and running systems in MathConnex. Other sources of information include the on-line Help system and the sample modules and projects provided with MathConnex, plus updates on MathSoft's World Wide Web site.

To open the on-line Help:

■ Choose **MathConnex Help** from the **Help** menu.

■ Use the Contents page to locate a topic in the Table of Contents. Use the Index and Search pages to search on a particular word or topic.

If you installed MathConnex with Mathcad 8 Professional, you can access sample MathConnex projects as follows:

■ Choose **Open** from the **File** menu.

■ Double-click the SAMPLES folder.

■ Select a project (.MXP file) and click "Open."

To access the sample MathConnex modules:

■ Click the Modules tab in the MathConnex Explorer.

■ Open the Sample Modules folder.

■ Drag and drop a module from the MathConnex Explorer to the Worksheet.

For updated information about MathConnex, including additional sample projects, visit MathSoft's World Wide Web site:

http://www.mathsoft.com/

Chapter 2
The MathConnex Workspace

The MathConnex workspace is your interface for accessing computational *components*, connecting components into *systems* in the MathConnex Worksheet, arranging and sharing systems and other OLE objects as MathConnex *projects*, and reusing *modules*.

This chapter has the following sections:

Starting MathConnex

What you see when you launch MathConnex.

Menus, Toolbar, and Status Bar

The MathConnex command interface.

Component palettes

Drag-and-drop interface for the basic MathConnex components.

The Worksheet

Where you create systems, projects, and modules.

The MathConnex Explorer

An interface for arranging available modules and components and for accessing the components in the current project.

Starting MathConnex

For information on system requirements and how to install MathConnex, see the instructions that accompanied your installation media.

If you installed MathConnex with Mathcad 8 Professional, you can start MathConnex by clicking ![icon] on Mathcad's Standard toolbar. When you launch MathConnex, you see the MathConnex workspace as shown in Figure 2-1.

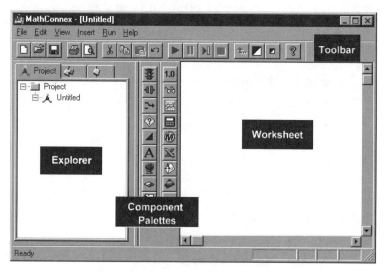

Figure 2-1: The MathConnex workspace.

The following sections introduce:

- Menu commands, the Toolbar, and the Status Bar.

- The two Component Palettes, your interface to the computational tools of Math-Connex.

- The Worksheet, where you create computational systems from components.

- The MathConnex Explorer, an object browser to manage projects and modules.

The Toolbar, Component Palettes, and Explorer can be resized, dragged off the application window, or docked (attached) to various borders of the MathConnex window. Use commands on the **View** menu to toggle the display of the Toolbar, Component Palettes, Status Bar, and Explorer.

Tip   You can undock a docked element of the workspace by double-clicking its border.

Menus, Toolbar, and Status Bar

Menu commands

File Menu

New	Begin a new MathConnex project.
Open...	Open an existing MathConnex project.
Save	Save a MathConnex project.
Save As...	Save a MathConnex project to a different filename.
Print Setup...	Define the properties for printing a project.
Print Preview	Display a replica of what the project will look like when it is printed.
Print...	Print the active project.
Send...	Attach a copy of the current project to an email message. The recipient of the mail must have properly installed MathConnex software to view the project.
Recent Files	Open most recently saved MathConnex projects.
Exit	Close MathConnex.

Edit Menu

Undo	Undo the last command.
Redo	Redo the last command.
Cut	Remove the selected object(s) from the Worksheet and place in the Clipboard.
Copy	Place a copy of the selected object(s) on the Clipboard.
Paste	Insert the contents of the Clipboard into the Worksheet.
Object	Activate embedded or linked object.

View Menu

Toolbar	Toggle the display of the Toolbar.
Status Bar	Toggle the display of the Status Bar.
Explorer	Toggle the display of the Explorer.
Component Palette 1	Toggle the display of ten built-in component buttons.

Component Palette 2	Toggle the display of ten built-in component buttons.
Go Back	Go to higher level of worksheet when a collapsed subsystem is being viewed.
Zoom In	Increase the scale of the Worksheet display to magnify the objects on the Worksheet.
Zoom Out	Decrease the scale of the Worksheet display to reduce the size of the objects on the Worksheet.
Show Labels	Toggle the display of labels on components in the Worksheet.

Insert Menu

Component...	Launch Wizard to insert component into the Worksheet.
Object...	Insert an OLE object into the Worksheet.
Scripted Object...	Launch Scripting Wizard to insert a scripted component into the Worksheet.

Run Menu

Run	Run the system contained in the Worksheet.
Pause	Pause a running system.
Step	Run the next component connected in the Worksheet.
Stop	Stop a running or paused system.
Single Step Mode	Toggle the execution of parallel systems to be sequential or concurrent. (See Chapter 5, "Advanced Topics.")
Highlight Components	Toggle the highlighting of the component currently being calculated during the run.

Help Menu

MathConnex Help...	Show MathConnex Help topics.
Tip of the Day	Display tips for using MathConnex.
About MathConnex...	Display program information, version number, and copyright.

Toolbar buttons

	New	Open blank Worksheet for a new MathConnex project.
	Open	Open an existing MathConnex project.
	Save	Save a MathConnex project to a .MXP file.
	Print	Print the active project.
	Print Preview	Display a replica of what the project will look like when it is printed.
	Cut	Remove the selected object(s) and place them in Clipboard.
	Copy	Send copy of the selected object(s) to Clipboard.
	Paste	Insert contents of Clipboard into Worksheet.
	Undo	Undo the last action.
	Run	Run the system contained in the Worksheet.
	Pause	Pause a running system.
	Step	Run the next component connected in the Worksheet.
	Stop	Stop a running or paused system.
	Back	Go to a higher-level worksheet.
	Zoom In	Increase the scale of the Worksheet.
	Zoom Out	Decrease the scale of the Worksheet.
	Help	Show MathConnex Help topics.

Status Bar

The Status Bar at the bottom of the window describes the current operation whenever you select a menu command. Look in the right-hand part of the Status Bar to see the *run mode* of the system you have on the Worksheet:

■ **RUN**—the system is currently executing

■ **PAUSE**—execution has been paused

■ **STOP**—execution has been stopped

Component palettes

MathConnex comes with a collection of built-in components, displayed on two palettes, for use in building systems. To insert a component from one of the Component Palettes:

■ Click and hold the left mouse button on a component in the Component Palettes.

■ Drag the component to the location you want in your Worksheet, and release the mouse button.

Components to generate, import, or export data

1.0	**Input**	Input a single value or an array in a scrollable table.
	File Read or Write	Input data from or output data to a file.
	Ramp	Generate a sequence of equally spaced values.
	Global Variable	Input a value accessible by any component in the system.

Components for viewing results

	Inspector	Inspect data values in a scrollable table.
	Graph	Graph data on a 2D plot.
	3D Plot	Graph data on a 3D plot.
	Axum	Display an Axum 2D or 3D plot, if Axum is installed on your system.
	S-PLUS Graph	Display an S-PLUS 2D or 3D plot, if S-PLUS is installed on your system

Computational components

	Mathcad	Compute with Mathcad, if installed on your system.
	S-PLUS Script	Compute with S-PLUS, if installed on your system
	Excel	Compute with Excel, if installed on your system.
.m	**MATLAB**	Compute with MATLAB, if installed on your system.
	ConnexScript	Compute using commands in the ConnexScript language.

Components for controlling data flow

	Conditional	Conditionally route data to output ports.
	Initialize	Take initial value from one input port and subsequent values from another.
	Wire Breaker	Break (interrupt) data flow along the wire.
	Stop or Pause	Pause or stop running a system.

Other components

	Text	Create text region for annotation.
	Scripted Object	Script a custom OLE Automation object.

Several components launch a Setup Wizard to guide you through initial configuration of input and output ports and other properties. For others, you must assign properties manually. For details on the components, see Chapter 4, "Components." The Scripted Object component is taken up in detail in Chapter 5, "Advanced Topics."

The Worksheet

In the Worksheet of MathConnex you:

- Design, run, analyze, and edit one or more MathConnex *systems*.

- Change your view by zooming or by collapsing *subsystems*.

- Annotate your MathConnex systems with text or other OLE objects.

- Save, print, or email the Worksheet contents as a MathConnex *project*, and save groups of configured, connected components as *modules*.

Systems

In MathConnex you have a single Worksheet to work with, although you may have as many systems on it as you like. As described on page 12, however, you can hide complexity in the Worksheet by collapsing a group of components into a subsystem, and a subsystem itself may have other subsystems. A Worksheet may therefore have a hierarchy of components.

Figure 2-2 shows a MathConnex system in the Worksheet that models a double pendulum. See Chapter 3, "Creating and Running a System," for a step-by-step example of creating a MathConnex system. You typically follow these steps in creating a system:

- Plan the components and external files that the system will need, and anticipate what the output of the system will be: a file, data to be viewed, a graph, etc.

- Place components on the Worksheet by dragging and dropping them from the Component Palettes, or by choosing **Component** from the **Insert** menu.

- Configure the components you have placed on the worksheet using options on the component pop-up menus. You access the pop-up menu for a component by clicking it with the *right* mouse button. You decide on the correct number of inputs and outputs for each and choose display properties and other options.

- Wire the components together, connecting an output port from one component to the input port of another, so that data flows correctly from component to component.

- Run and stop the system, using the ![play], ![pause], ![step], and ![stop] Toolbar buttons or the corresponding commands on the **Run** menu.

- Modify the system as needed: change the properties of components, change the wiring of components, or change the data sources or data outputs.

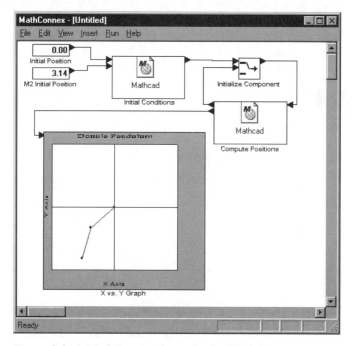

Figure 2-2: A MathConnex system in the Worksheet.

Changing your view on the Worksheet

Because systems with more than a few components may be too complex to view easily on the screen, MathConnex provides several ways to simplify or change the view of your Worksheet. You can:

- Scroll to view a different part of the Worksheet, using the scrollbars.

- Zoom in and out of areas on the Worksheet, using the ▣ and ▣ Toolbar buttons or the corresponding **View** menu commands.

- Collapse the display of one or more components into a *subsystem* on your Worksheet. In this way you hide or nest details about the components in your system and create an additional *level* in the Worksheet.

Creating a subsystem

To create a subsystem in your system, select one or more components in the Worksheet, click the selected components with the right mouse button to see the pop-up menu, and choose **Collapse**.

You may create as many levels as you like in your Worksheet by collapsing component groups. MathConnex displays a collapsed subsystem using a subsystem icon in the Worksheet, but the components in the subsystem continue to have the properties and connections they had before you collapsed the view. The system runs exactly as it did before you collapsed the components.

To see and edit the contents of the subsystem, double-click the subsystem icon ▣, which opens up a new Worksheet level containing the components of the subsystem but in which other components of the system aren't editable. MathConnex displays the

▣ icon in this view to indicate that the system contains components at other levels. To return to the Worksheet level in which the subsystem displays as an icon, choose

Go Back on the **View** menu or click the ▣ Toolbar button.

Locking a subsystem

You can *lock* a subsystem so its contents can only be viewed and edited after a password is entered. To do so, click the subsystem icon with the right mouse button and choose **Lock** from the pop-up menu. Enter a password in the dialog box. You will be prompted for the password the next time you try to view the contents of the subsystem.

When you create a subsystem, and especially if you have locked it, you'll usually want to leave any components in it hidden when you run the system. To view a particular subsystem component in a higher Worksheet level, however, do the following:

- Open the subsystem containing that component as described above.

- Click the component with the right mouse button.

- Choose **View⇒In Parent** from the pop-up menu.

Now when you go back to the higher Worksheet level, you see the corresponding component in place of the icon that otherwise denotes a collapsed subsystem. However, the component may only be edited in the Worksheet level it came from.

To restore a subsystem to its uncollapsed appearance, click the subsystem icon in the Worksheet with the right mouse button and choose **Expand** from the pop-up menu.

Annotating the Worksheet

The use of labels on components and modifying the appearance of components with icons or other OLE objects are described in "Changing the appearance of components" on page 35. In addition to these options, MathConnex lets you annotate your Worksheet so that you can document your project and communicate your results to others. You can annotate the Worksheet with:

■ Text regions created with the Text component.

■ OLE objects from other applications on your system.

Text

The Text component lets you place an editable, scrolling region on the Worksheet containing any text you choose and displayed with a variety of formatting options. You place the Text component on the Worksheet by dragging

The Mathcad component in the system takes a 3 by 3 array input and computes the eigenvalues and eigenvectors of the matrix

A from the Component Palettes. Then start typing text in the region.

The Text component is comparable in functionality to the text annotation tool in Microsoft Paint (an accessory normally found in Microsoft Windows). See Chapter Chapter 4, "Components," for details.

OLE objects

The MathConnex Worksheet is a versatile OLE 2 container, so you can embed or link objects created by other OLE-compatible applications on your system. For example, you can embed a document created by Microsoft Word to describe the systems in the Worksheet, and double-click on the embedded document to activate Microsoft Word in-place for editing.

You can place an OLE object in the Worksheet in one of several ways. For example:

■ Simply drag an object from an OLE 2–compatible application on your system and drop it onto the MathConnex Worksheet. This embeds an object in the Worksheet.

■ Choose **Object** from the **Insert** menu.

When you choose **Object** from the **Insert** menu, Math-Connex displays a dialog box listing available OLE servers on your system. You have three options:

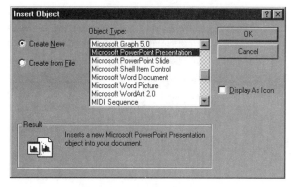

■ Click Create New to create a *new* object directly in the Worksheet.

■ Click Create from File and browse to find a file to *embed* an object in the Worksheet. An embedded object does not update automatically when the source file changes, but you can double-click it to activate it for editing.

■ Click Create from File, browse to find a file, and check Link to *link* to an object. Here, changes to the source file are reflected automatically in the object.

Projects and modules

MathConnex is an interactive environment for creating computational systems, but you can save your work, or portions of it, to edit or re-use at a later date, as well as share your systems and components with others. You can save:

■ A MathConnex *project*, which is a working snapshot of all the systems and other objects in the MathConnex Worksheet.

■ A MathConnex *module*, which is a preconfigured, prewired group of components.

Projects

To save your work as a MathConnex project, choose **Save** from the **File** menu, or click

![save icon] on the Toolbar. To save an existing MathConnex project under a different name, choose **Save As** from the **File** menu.

Note MathConnex uses .MXP as the default extension for MathConnex projects.

To print a MathConnex project, choose **Print** from the **File** menu, or click ![print icon] on the Toolbar. The **Print Preview** command on the **File** menu allows you to view, scroll, and zoom your printed output before you send it to the printer. Use **Print Setup** on the **File** menu to choose and configure an available printer, select a paper size and source, and choose either portrait or landscape orientation for your printed output.

To send a MathConnex project as an attachment to an email message from a MAPI-compliant mail application such as Microsoft Mail, choose **Send** from the **File** menu. Your mail program launches with a blank message containing the current project as an attachment but waiting for you fill in the recipient, title, and other information.

Modules

To save a component or group of components to re-use in other MathConnex systems:

■ Drag-select one or more components, or an entire system, in the Worksheet.

■ Click with the right mouse button on one of the selected components.

■ Choose **Save as Module** from the pop-up menu, which displays the Name Module dialog box shown below.

■ Enter a brief, descriptive name and other information about the module.

■ Click "OK." MathConnex saves the module in a default location.

As described on page 17, you access, rename, import, and export available modules via the Modules tab in the Explorer.

The MathConnex Explorer

The MathConnex Explorer is an object browser for organizing the projects, modules, and components you can work with in MathConnex. The three tabs in the Explorer give you a tree display of:

■ The contents of the project currently in the Worksheet.

■ Available modules in your copy of MathConnex.

■ Available components in your copy of MathConnex.

Project tab

As you build a project in the Worksheet, the tree diagram in the Project tab expands to show the components you have used. Similarly, when you open an existing MathConnex project, all the components in the Worksheet are listed in the tree diagram. Although the project tree lists components but not the connections between them, it can be extremely useful for navigating large projects.

If you click on a component name in the project tree, the corresponding component in the Worksheet is surrounded with a selection box.

Tip Click the right mouse button on a component name in the project tree to access options for deleting, editing (activating), and assigning properties to the component in the Worksheet.

Modules tab

The Modules tab in the Explorer arranges available modules you can use in the Worksheet. Folders of modules are listed alphabetically, and modules within them are listed alphabetically by the names assigned to them in the Name Module dialog box.

When you want to use a module, simply drag and drop one of the modules listed here into the Worksheet.

To move a module into a different folder, drag it there.

MathConnex is shipped with a set of modules you can find in the Sample Modules folder.

Tip To create a new subfolder in the Module tab, click with the right mouse button component on one of the folders and choose **New Folder** from the pop-up menu. Also use this pop-up menu to delete or rename a folder.

Exporting and importing modules

When you create a module, MathConnex saves it automatically for you in the `modules` folder of the location where you installed Mathcad and MathConnex. The module is added automatically to the tree in the Modules tab using whatever name you supplied in the Name Module dialog box.

To share a module with someone else, first export it by clicking on the module name with the right mouse button and choosing **Export** from the pop-up menu. You are prompted for a location to save the Mathconnex module file.

Note MathConnex uses .MXM as the default extension for exported MathConnex module files.

To import a module file so that you can use it in your MathConnex workspace, click with the right mouse button on a folder name in the Module tab and choose **Import** from the pop-up menu. Select a .MXM file from the dialog box. The module then appears in the Modules tab.

Components tab

The Components tab lists shortcuts for available Math-Connex components.

By default the Components tab has a MathConnex Components folder that lists all the components that were installed at the time you installed MathConnex. But you can arrange the components into any folders you want to; you add, delete, and rename folders in this tab just as you do in the Modules tab of the MathConnex Explorer.

As an alternative to dragging and dropping one of the basic components from the Component Palettes, you can drag and drop one of the components listed here into the Worksheet.

To move a component to a different folder in the Components tab, simply drag it there.

Adding and deleting components

When you install MathConnex, all components that ship with the product are installed at that time and are available for use via the Component Palettes or the Components tab. You may later install components from MathSoft or other sources and want to be able to drag and drop them from the Explorer's Component tab into the Worksheet.

To add a component to one of the folders in the Components tab, click with the right mouse button on a folder and choose **Add Component** from the pop-up menu. The Components dialog box lists components that have been installed. Choose one of the listed components in the dialog box to add a shortcut in the Components tab. You may add as many shortcuts to a component as you like.

To delete a component from the tree, click with the right mouse button on one of the components in the Components tab and choose **Delete** from the pop-up menu or press the [**Del**] key.

Note   Deleting a component from the tree in the Components tab does not physically delete the component from MathConnex. You can add it back later to the Components tab via the **Add Component** command.

Chapter 3
Creating and Running a System

This chapter teaches you how to use MathConnex to create and run a multicomponent system. The focus of the chapter is an example system in which data is brought into Mathcad for polynomial regression.

Overview

General information on creating a system.

Placing components on the Worksheet

Dragging and dropping components from the Component Palettes to the Worksheet.

Getting organized

Moving, copying and pasting, and deleting components. Resizing a component. Flipping the direction of a component's ports.

Configuring the components

Using the Properties dialog to label and configure a component. Using other pop-up menu options. Activating a component to edit it.

Wiring components together

Connecting and disconnecting components with wires.

Running and stopping a system

The basics of running and stopping a system. Highlighting active components. Stepping through a system component by component. Pausing a running system. Making a system run up to a certain component. Observing values as they pass through a wire.

Changing the appearance of components

Viewing a component as an icon or as another object. Showing labels.

Overview

MathConnex lets you design systems of applications and data sources where each application and data source is a *component* in the system. The components are wired together so that when you run the system, data flows from one component to the next; the output data from one component becomes the input data for the next component. What each component does with the data as it passes through is determined by the type of component and how it is configured.

To create a system, you should first determine which components you'd like to use. See page 10 for a brief description of each of the available components. Refer to Chapter 4, "Components," for detailed information.

Once you've determined what components to use in a system, you will:

- Place the components on the Worksheet by dragging and dropping them from the Component Palettes.

- Arrange them appropriately on the Worksheet.

- Configure each component so that it knows what do with the data it receives and what data to send to the next component.

- Wire the components together by connecting the output port of one component to the input port of another.

- Run the system.

A completed system might look like this:

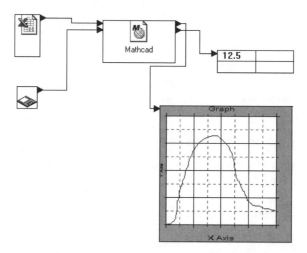

This chapter explains each of the steps involved in creating a system and describes a sample system for you to create, if you have Mathcad 8 Professional available. It also discusses how to customize the appearance of a component in your project.

The example

In the sample system we will design in this chapter, data stored in an external data file is passed into a Mathcad worksheet. The Mathcad worksheet performs a second-order polynomial regression on the data and finds the coefficients of the second-order polynomial that best fits the data. Mathcad passes the coefficients and the value of R^2, indicating how closely the data fit the polynomial, back into the system. The components involved in this system are:

■ An Input component, for bringing in the data.

■ A Mathcad component, for performing the polynomial regression.

■ Two instances of the Inspector component, for displaying the coefficients and R^2.

We will place these components on the Worksheet, configure them, wire them together, and run the system.

Tip If you installed MathConnex with Mathcad 8 Professional, the MathConnex project CURVEFIT.MXP located in the SAMPLES folder shows a completed version of this example. To see more sophisticated examples involving a wider variety of components, browse the sample MathConnex projects located in the SAMPLES folder.

Although this example is fairly simple, it illustrates how you can use MathConnex to connect other applications and data sources to each other and pass data from one component to another. For instance, you can pass values into Mathcad from an Excel component, or you can send results from Mathcad to a MATLAB component, or to another Mathcad component, or to a data file. You can use the Conditional component to use different sets of data depending on whether the results satisfy a certain condition. The number of possible systems you can create and their complexity are unlimited.

Placing components on the Worksheet

You can place components for a system on your MathConnex Worksheet by dragging and dropping them from the Component Palettes:

■ Click the icon for the component in the Component Palettes.

■ Hold the left mouse button down.

■ Drag the icon to the Worksheet.

■ Let go of the mouse button.

You will immediately see the component inserted into the Worksheet, or you will see a Setup Wizard dialog that walks you through initial configuration of the component.

For example, place the Input component on your Worksheet using these steps:

■ Drag the  icon from the Component Palettes to your Worksheet. The Input component appears:

Place two copies of the Inspector component on your Worksheet using similar steps:

■ Drag the ⬛ icon from the Component Palettes to your Worksheet. The Inspector component appears:

■ Drag the ⬛ icon from the Component Palettes to your Worksheet again to insert
another Inspector component.

Place the Mathcad component on your Worksheet:

■ Make sure Mathcad 8 Professional is installed (but not necessarily running) on your
system.

■ Drag the ⬛ icon from
the Component Palettes to
your Worksheet. This
launches the Mathcad Set-
up Wizard. This dialog box
lets you specify whether
you want to create a new
Mathcad worksheet or use
an existing one. For this
example, we will use an
existing worksheet that already has the necessary
curve fitting equations entered in it.

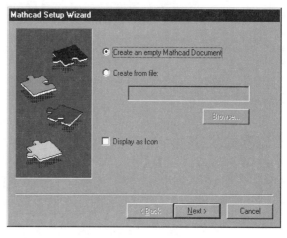

■ Click "Create from file" and browse to find the file CRVFIT.MCD in the SAMPLES
folder.

■ Click "Open."

■ Check Display as Icon This inserts the Mathcad component as an icon instead of
as a window on the Worksheet so we won't have to see all the curve fitting equations.

■ Click "Next." The next page of the Wizard lets you specify the number of inputs
and outputs. For this example, we will pass one set of data to the Mathcad
component as input and we will send two sets of data out of the Mathcad component
as output.

■ Specify 1 input and 2 outputs.

■ Click "Finish."

When you finish using the Wizard, you'll see an iconified Mathcad component in your Worksheet with one input port and two output ports:

Now you should see the Input component, two Inspector components, and the Mathcad component somewhere in your Worksheet, as shown below:

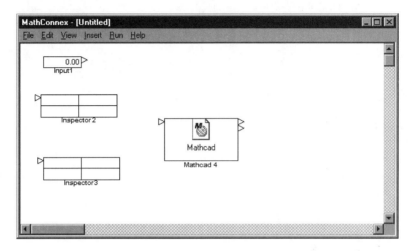

Once you've placed components on a Worksheet, you can move them around, resize them, or flip their port directions so that they fit best on the Worksheet. The following sections describe each of these operations in more detail.

Moving a Component

To move a component:

■ Click a component to select it.

■ Hold down the left mouse button and drag the component to a new spot in the Worksheet. Any connecting wires adjust accordingly (although you may not have any at this point).

Try moving the Input, Mathcad, and Inspector components so that they are arranged this way:

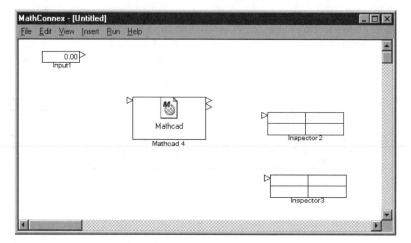

Moving multiple components

To move several components and maintain their connections:

■ Position the mouse pointer outside the components you want to move.

■ Hold the left mouse button down and drag a box around all the components you want to move.

■ Release the mouse button.

■ Click any of the components, hold the mouse button down, and drag the component around the Worksheet. All the other components move with it. Any connecting wires adjust accordingly.

Resizing a component

You can see more or less of a component or you can stretch it. For example, to resize the Input component so that you see more of the table cells:

■ Double-click the component to activate it. Handles appear on the sides of the component.

■ Move the cursor to one of the handles until it changes to a double-headed arrow.

■ Hold the left mouse button down and drag the cursor in the direction you want the component's dimensions to change.

- Release the mouse button.

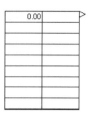

To stretch a component:

- Click once to select it (but not to activate it). Handles appear on the sides of the component.

- Move the cursor to any of the until it changes to a double-headed arrow.

- Hold the left mouse button down and drag the cursor in the direction you want the component's dimensions to change.

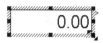

- Release the mouse button.

To return a component to its original size after stretching it:

- Click the component with the right mouse button.

- Choose **View**⇒**Original Size** from the pop-up menu.

Adding and removing ports

When you place a component on a Worksheet, it has a certain number of input ports and a certain number of output ports, either by default or according to what you specified in a Wizard. You can modify the number of ports on some components.

To add or remove ports:

- Click the component with the right mouse button.

- Choose **Add Input Port, Add Output Port**, **Remove Input Port**, or **Remove Output Port** from the pop-up menu.

Flipping port direction

By default, any input ports a component has are located on its left side and any output ports are located on its right side. You can reverse these port directions. Reversing the port directions may reduce a system's apparent complexity by shortening the wire paths between connected components.

To flip the port direction of a component:

- Click the component with the right mouse button.

- Choose **Flip Port Direction** from the pop-up menu. The input and output ports on the component change direction, and any connecting wires adjust accordingly.

Note The **Flip Port Direction** menu item toggles the port direction. Selecting it again returns the ports to their original orientation.

Deleting components

To remove a component from the Worksheet:

- Click a component to select it.

- Press [**Del**].

To remove multiple components:

- Position the mouse pointer outside the components you want to delete.

- Hold the left mouse button down and drag a box around all the components you want to delete.

- Release the mouse button.

- Press [**Del**].

Copying, cutting, and pasting components

To copy or cut a component from a Worksheet:

- Click a component to select it, or select a group of components by holding the left mouse button down and dragging over all the components you want to select.

- Click [icon] or [icon] on the Toolbar or choose **Copy** or **Cut** from the **Edit** menu to copy or cut the component to the Clipboard.

- Click on any blank area of the Worksheet.

- Click [icon] on the Toolbar or choose **Paste** from the **Edit** menu. A copy of the component(s) on the Clipboard is inserted at the upper left corner of the Worksheet.

- If necessary, move the copied component to another location in the Worksheet.

Configuring the components

After inserting components into a Worksheet, you configure each component so that it knows what to do with the input and what to send as output. To do so, you use the Properties dialog for the component, apply other commands from the component's pop-up menu, or enter values or equations directly into the component.

Using the Properties dialog

Some components, such as the Mathcad component, are inserted into the Worksheet via a Setup Wizard, so you will already have done some configuration when you insert them. Other components, however, must be configured via the Properties dialog box. To do so:

- Click a component with the right (or second) mouse button. A pop-up menu appears.

- Choose **Properties**. You'll see a tabbed dialog box, like the one shown at right for the Inspector component.

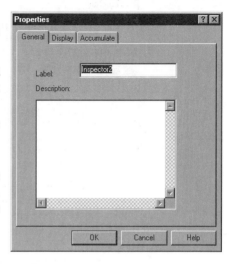

Many options that control the behavior of a component are available in this dialog box. Each component has a General tab showing the component's label—the name that appears below the component—and a brief description, if you choose, of what the component does.

Since this Inspector component in our example will be displaying the coefficients Mathcad calculates, rename it "Coefficients" as follows:

- Type **Coefficients** in the Label text box.

- Click "OK."

Try relabeling the other components in the system using the General tab in the Properties dialog of each component:

- Label the other Inspector component **R-squared**.

- Label the Mathcad component **Curve fit**.

- Label the Input component **Data**.

The other tabs in the Properties dialog box differ for each component. For information on the options for a particular component, see Chapter 4, "Components." For example, to find out more about the options in the Display and Accumulate tabs for the Inspector component's Properties dialog, see page 49.

Using other options from the pop-up menu

The **Properties** command from a component's pop-up menu is one way to control how it is going to behave or appear in a system. Other commands on the pop-up menu control other characteristics of a component's behavior.

In our example, we need to import data from a data file into the Input component. To do that, we need to use the **Import** command from the Input component's pop-up menu:

■ Click the Input component with the right mouse button.

■ Choose **Import** from the pop-up menu. You'll see the Read From File dialog box. This dialog box lets you specify the name and type of file to import. For this example, we will import a Microsoft Excel data file.

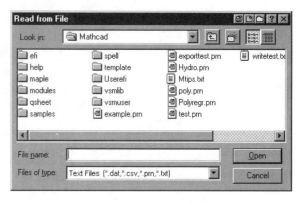

■ Choose Excel Files from the "Files of Type" drop-down list.

■ Browse to the file CRVDATA.XLS located in the SAMPLES folder.

■ Click "Open."

The cells of the Input component are filled with data values for our curve-fitting procedure. The first column contains the *x*-values and the second column contains the *y*-values.

10.00	25.20
10.00	27.30
10.00	28.70
15.00	29.80
15.00	31.10
15.00	27.80
20.00	31.20
20.00	32.60
20.00	29.70
25.00	31.70

Data

Activating a component

To type equations or values into a component, to resize it, or to scroll through it, you first need to double-click it to activate it. Some components activate in-place: the MathConnex menus and tool bars change automatically to those specific to the component, and scrollbars and handles appear on the edges of the component.

For example, to activate the Input component, double-click it. You'll see:

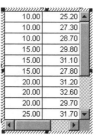

■ Scrollbars for scrolling around the values in the component.

■ Handles for resizing.

You'll also have access to the cells in the table.

Other components, and components displayed as icons, activate in a separate window rather than in place. For example, to activate the Mathcad component:

■ Double-click it.

You'll see a Mathcad window containing the Mathcad worksheet and giving you access to the equations in it. Figure 3-1 shows an example.

Here you can see that:

- The curve fit is performed by the Mathcad *regress* function.

- The data going into Mathcad is passed to the Mathcad variable **in0** and the outputs are values from the Mathcad variables **out0** and **out1**. These names are always associated with the inputs and outputs of a Mathcad component. See page 62 for more information.

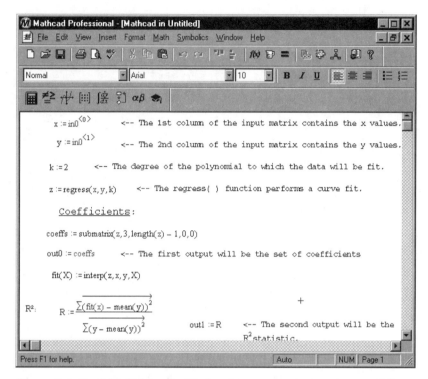

Figure 3-1: Double-clicking the Mathcad component icon activates a full Mathcad window.

Note Since the Mathcad component is displayed as an icon in this example, double-clicking it brings up a separate window. If the component were displayed as a Mathcad worksheet, however, double-clicking it would activate Mathcad in-place: the MathConnex menus and tool bars would be replaced with those of Mathcad.

Wiring components together

Once you've placed two or more components on your Worksheet and configured them, you can wire them together so that the data flows from one to the next. See Figure 3-2 for an example.

To wire two components together:

- Position the pointer over the output port from one component until it changes to a .

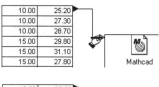

- Click and hold the left mouse button and drag to the input port of another component.

- When the pointer changes to a [icon], release the mouse button. The connected input and output ports now are shaded black.

Note You can connect wires either from–to or to–from components. You can also connect multiple wires from one output port, but only one wire can enter an input port.

You can connect the output ports of the Mathcad component to the input ports of the Inspector components so that you have a system that looks like Figure 3-2.

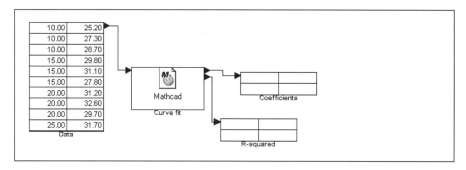

Figure 3-2: A completed curve-fitting system. The Mathcad component calculates a polynomial fit for the data and outputs the results.

Disconnecting components

If you need to disconnect two components:

- Move the pointer over the input port of a component to which a wire is attached. The pointer changes to ⬚.

- Click the left mouse button and hold it down while moving to an empty area of the Worksheet.

- When the pointer changes to a crosshair, release the mouse button. The wire disappears.

Note   A wire can be disconnected from an input port only. If you drag a wire from an output port, you create another wire.

Tip   If you disconnect a wire by mistake, choose **Undo** from the **Edit** menu or type [**Ctrl**]**Z** to reconnect the wire.

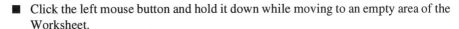

Running and stopping a system

After placing a group of components on a Worksheet and connecting them, you can make data flow from one to the next by running the system.

The basics

To run a system:

- Choose **Run** from the **Run** menu or press ▶ on the Toolbar.

When you run a system, data flows from one component to the next until the system is stopped. Even if data has reached its final destination, a system keeps running until you choose to stop it. For more information on the run model MathConnex follows, see Chapter 5, "Advanced Topics."

To stop data from flowing through the system, you can:

- Choose **Stop** from the **Run** menu.

- Press ■ on the Toolbar.

- Place a Stop/Pause component at the end of a system.

Placing a Stop/Pause component at the end of a system is generally the best way to stop a system, since it eliminates the need for you to stop a system manually each time it runs. For more information on the Stop/Pause component, see page 75.

Note Until you stop a system, you are unable to edit your project or drag components from the Component Palettes.

Figure 3-3 shows a system that ran and was stopped using the **Stop** command. Data passed from the Input component to the Mathcad component. The Mathcad component calculated the curve fit and passed the coefficients to one Inspector component and the value of R^2 to the other.

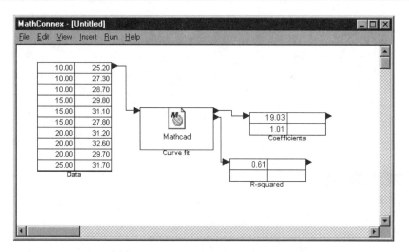

*Figure 3-3: Running a completed curve-fitting system. Choose **Run** and then **Stop** from the **Run** menu.*

Highlighting active components

As data flows into a component, it starts processing. If you want to see which components are processing as the data flows through a system:

■ Choose **Highlight Components** from the **Run** menu.

■ Run the system.

As each component becomes active, its border turns green.

Stepping through a system

If you want to see a system run component by component, you can step through a system. To do so:

■ Choose **Highlight Components** from the **Run** menu.

■ Choose **Step** repeatedly from the **Run** menu or continually press [icon] on the Toolbar.

The system runs through one component at a time, and the borders of the currently active components are highlighted in green. When you step through the curve-fitting system shown in Figure 3-2, you'll see that first the Constant component is active, then the Mathcad component, and then the two Inspector components.

In our example, it is easy to determine the order in which the components become active. In a more complicated example, however, a system can branch when a component can send output to more than one component. In a case such as this, the **Highlight Components** option is especially helpful.

Pausing a running system

To stop a running system temporarily:

- Press ⏸ on the Toolbar, or choose **Pause** from the **Run** menu, while the system is running.

- The system pauses until you resume running it by clicking ▶ or ▶⏸ on the Toolbar.

Note You can also pause a system by placing a Stop/Pause component in it. For more information on the Stop/Pause component, see page 75.

Tip While the system is paused, you can view input data on the wires using the magnifying glass. See page 34 for more information.

Breakpoints

Adding a breakpoint to your system allows you to analyze your system by examining the values at a prespecified point in the system rather than pausing the system at random. You can add and remove breakpoints to individual components or to all the components in a system.

Adding breakpoints

To add a breakpoint to a component:

- Click the component with the right mouse button to display the component's pop-up menu.

- Choose **Add Breakpoint** from the pop-up menu. The component is outlined in red.

- Run the system.

The component's border turns yellow each time the breakpoint is reached when you run the system.

Clicking ▶⏸ or ▶ on the Toolbar after the temporary breakpoint has been triggered continues execution and removes the temporary breakpoint.

To add a breakpoint to all the components in a system:

- Click in a blank spot of the Worksheet with the right mouse button to display a pop-up menu.

- Choose **Set All Breakpoints** from the pop-up menu. All the components are outlined in red.

Removing breakpoints

To remove a breakpoint from a component:

- Click the component with the right mouse button to display the component's pop-up menu.

- Choose **Remove Breakpoint** from the pop-up menu. The red outline disappears.

To remove all the breakpoints in a system at once:

- Click in a blank spot of the Worksheet with the right mouse button to display a pop-up menu.

- Choose **Remove All Breakpoints** from the pop-up menu. The red outlines on all components disappear.

Running to a particular point

To run a system up to a predefined component in the Worksheet:

- Click the component with the right mouse button to see the component's pop-up menu.

- Choose **Run to This Point** from the pop-up menu. The component is outlined in red.

The system automatically runs until it reaches the component. At this point, execution pauses and the component's border turns green.

You can resume running the Worksheet by clicking [▶|] or [▶] on the Toolbar.

Inspecting values as they pass through the system

As a system is running, you can see what values are on a wire, either out of an output port or into an input port. To do so:

- Choose **Pause** from the **Run** menu.

- Let the mouse pointer hover over a component's output port until it changes to [🔍]. The value being passed out of the component appears.

- Move the pointer over a component's input port to see the value being passed into the component.

- If the value being passed is a vector or matrix, click with the left mouse button while the [🔍] is showing to see a tabular display of the vector or matrix.

Changing the appearance of components

When you place a component on a Worksheet, it has a certain default appearance. For example, the Inspector component by default shows a 2×2 spreadsheet-like table.

In some systems, you can minimize the amount of space a component takes up or otherwise alter the appearance of a component. You can change the way a component appears in a MathConnex Worksheet by resizing the component, displaying it as an icon, or displaying another object in place of it.

When you change the appearance of a component, keep in mind that you are not modifying the component's properties or the number of input and output ports. The component will behave as it did before you changed its appearance. You can also manipulate the component's properties and functionality just as you did before.

Displaying a component as an icon

By default, some components are designed to show calculations or certain property settings when they are inserted. For example, the Conditional component defaults to displaying all the conditional statements. In some cases, the appearance of the statements can make a system look cumbersome or needlessly complicated.

One way to hide the calculations or statements behind a component is to display the component as an icon. For example, to hide the data in the curve-fitting system shown in Figure 3-2, you can display the Input component as an icon:

- Click the component with the right mouse button to bring up its pop-up menu.

- Check **View⇒As Icon**. You'll see a default icon that is similar to the component's icon in the Component Palettes.

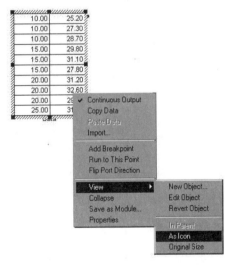

MathConnex chooses a default icon when you display a component as an icon. To change the icon to another available choice, click the object, choose **Object⇒Convert** from the **Edit** menu, check "Display as Icon," and choose "Change Icon." Select a different icon from the available choices.

If later you want to display the component in its default form again:

- Click the component with the right mouse button to bring up its pop-up menu.

- Uncheck **View⇒As Icon**.

Displaying a component as another object

In some cases, you may want the appearance of a component to indicate the component's behavior. For example, a component that simulates a circuit's behavior could show a diagram of the corresponding circuit. In this case, a diagram would be clearer than the component's default appearance or an icon. MathConnex therefore lets you view a component as some other object that's more appropriate.

In the sample system shown in Figure 3-3, the Input component provides data on the compressive strength of an alloy at various concentrations of an additive. Instead of displaying the actual data or an icon, you could substitute a picture of the alloy involved or of the instruments used to gather the data.

To do so:

- Click the component with the right mouse button to bring up its pop-up menu.

- Choose **View⇒New Object**.

- Choose an appropriate object in the Insert Object dialog box. For example, to create a new picture, select Bitmap Image to bring up Paint or another drawing application. If the application supports in-place activation, you'll see the MathConnex menus and toolbars change to the other application's menus and toolbars.

- Create the new object. When you are finished, click away from the component. The component's appearance will change to that of the object you created.

Once you create this object, you can edit it whenever you need to. In the example described above, for instance, you could to improve your drawing or add color.

To edit the object:

- Click the component with the right mouse button to bring up its pop-up menu.

- Choose **View⇒Edit Object**. The object activates in-place or inside the application that created it.

- Make the necessary changes.

- Click away from the component to resume working in MathConnex.

If, after viewing a component as an object, you want view it in its default form:

- Click the component with the right mouse button.

- Choose **View⇒Revert Object** from the pop-up menu.

Labeling a component

By default, when you place a component on a Worksheet, it displays a label at the bottom. The label indicates the type of component it is and the order in which you placed it on the Worksheet.

You can hide all labels in MathConnex, or you can change a component's label to something more appropriate for your system. For example,"Using the Properties dialog" on page 27 describes how to change the label of the Mathcad component to "Curvefit" instead of "Mathcad1" because the equations in the Mathcad component were performing a polynomial fit.

To change the label of a component:

■ Click the component with the right mouse button to bring up the pop-up menu.

■ Choose **Properties**.

■ Type a new label in the Label text box on the General page.

■ Click "OK."

To hide the labels of all components in the system:

■ Uncheck **Show Labels** from the **View** menu.

Chapter 4
Components

Every project you create in MathConnex consists of components, which you wire together to form a system. This chapter describes the basic MathConnex components in detail, explaining how each component generates or manipulates data and describing situations to use it.

Overview

General description of components, how to insert them into a Worksheet, and how to prepare them to pass data through a system.

Components for generating, importing, and exporting data

Using the Input component to type in data or import it from a file. Using the File Read/Write component to dynamically read from or write to a data file. Using the Ramp component to generate a series of data points. Using the Global Variable component to give a name to a set of data.

Components for viewing results

Using the Inspector component to view data in a table. Using the Graph, 3D Plot, Axum, and S-PLUS Graph components to graph data.

Computational components

Using the Mathcad, S-PLUS Script, Excel, MATLAB, and ConnexScript components to manipulate data mathematically.

Components for controlling data flow

Using the Conditional component to send data based on whether a conditional statement is true or false. Using the Initialize component to get data from one input port for the first execution and another port for all subsequent executions. Using the Stop/Pause component to halt a running system. Using the Wire Breaker component to prevent data flow from one component to another.

Other components

Using the Text component to annotate a project and describe a system. Introduction to the Scripted Object component for scripting an OLE object.

Overview

MathConnex lets you design systems of applications and data sources where each application and data source is a *component* in the system. A MathConnex Worksheet is therefore made up of various components connected to each other so that data flows from one component to the next. When data is flowing into a component, it is considered *input* to that component. Data coming out of a component is *output*.

Each component in a system does something different with the data. Some components generate data, others manipulate it as it passes through, and some components simply display the data or direct the data flow more precisely.

To create a system you should first determine which components you'd like to use in the system. Then you should:

■ Insert the necessary components onto a MathConnex Worksheet.

■ Configure each component so that it knows what do with the input and what to send as output.

■ Wire the components together, connecting the output port(s) of one component to the input port(s) of another.

■ Run the system.

Although the details of these steps differ slightly for every system you create, the sections that follow introduce the available components so that you know what they do, how to insert them, and how to configure them. See Chapter 3, "Creating and Running a System," for information on wiring components and running the system.

Inserting a component

In general, to insert one of the basic components into a MathConnex Worksheet:

■ Click a component icon from the Component Palettes.

■ Hold the mouse button down and drag the component to the Worksheet.

■ Release the mouse button.

Depending on the component you choose, you may see a Setup Wizard that lets you specify some properties of the component before it is inserted. Pressing "Next" continues through the Wizard. You can use the "Back" buttons to go back to a previous page. When you click "Finish," the component is inserted into your Worksheet.

If you don't see a Wizard when you drag one of the components onto the Worksheet, you'll immediately see the component, with some default properties, inserted into your Worksheet. For example, when

you drag the icon to the Worksheet, you'll see the Conditional component shown at right.

Each component has its own distinctive appearance, and each component has *input ports* and/or *output ports* that allow data to flow in and/or data to flow out of the component.

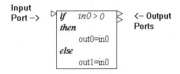

An input port allows data to pass into a component. An output port lets a component send data out. Some components have a fixed number of input ports and output ports, while other components can have up to four input ports and/or output ports. To add or remove input or output ports:

■ Click the component with the right mouse button to bring up the component's pop-up menu.

■ Choose **Add Input Port**, **Remove Input Port**, **Add Output Port**, or **Remove Output Port**.

Tip   You can also insert a component by choosing **Component** from the **Insert** menu and selecting a component from the list in the Wizard.

Controlling how a component appears in the Worksheet

Although each component has a default appearance, you can display some of the components as icons instead.

To display a component as an icon:

■ Click the component once to select it.

■ Click it with the right mouse button to see a pop-up menu.

■ Check **View⇒As Icon**.

The component appears as an icon in the Worksheet but maintains its previous functionality. This is useful when you don't need to see the details of a component's behavior. For example, if you do not want to see all the Excel values stored in an Excel component, you can view it as an icon.

By default, when you place a component on a Worksheet, it has a label at the bottom. The label indicates the type of component it is and the order in which you placed it on the Worksheet.

You can force MathConnex to hide these labels or you can change the label to something more appropriate for your system. To change the label of a component:

■ Right-click the component to bring up the pop-up menu.

■ Choose **Properties**.

■ In the General tab, type a new label in the Label text box.

To hide the component labels:

- Uncheck **Show Labels** from the **View** menu.

For more information on changing the appearance of a component by viewing it as another OLE object, see page 35.

Configuring a component

Once you've inserted a component into a Worksheet, you usually need to configure the component's properties so that the component knows how to handle any inputs it's getting from other components and what to send as output. To configure the properties for a component:

- Click the component once to select it.

- Click it with the right mouse button to bring up a pop-up menu, like the one shown here for the Inspector component.

Tip   To see the pop-up menu for any component, the component must not be activated. You can deactivate a component by clicking in a blank spot of the Worksheet.

- Choose **Properties** from the pop-up menu. The Properties dialog box for the component appears. The settings in the Properties dialog box differ for each component. For example, the properties dialog for the Excel component (shown at right) lets you specify the cells in which the input values are stored and the cells from which the outputs are sent.

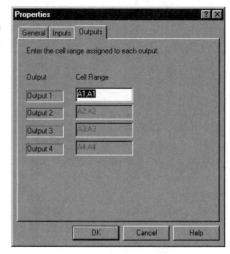

Final steps

Once you insert and configure a group of components on a Worksheet in MathConnex, you can wire them together and run the system. Refer to Chapter 3, "Creating and Running a System," for a step-by-step example of connecting components and running a system.

Components for generating, importing, and exporting data

Some components in MathConnex are useful for bringing data into or out of a system. A component that introduces data into a system might be used first in a system. Components that export data to a data file or to the Clipboard are useful whenever you need to capture the results for later use.

When you work with these data components, you should consider where the data is stored:

■ If your data is stored in a data file, you can use the Input component or the File Read/Write component to read it into MathConnex.

■ If you need to enter your data manually or import it from the Clipboard, use the Input component.

■ Use the Ramp component to generate a series of data values.

■ The File Read/Write component can dynamically write data to a variety of data file types.

■ The Global Variable component is useful for referring to some data produced anywhere in the system so you don't have to connect to the actual component producing it.

Input

Using the Input component you can:

■ Enter data manually so it can be used in a system.

■ Import data from a data file.

■ Paste in data from the Clipboard.

To place the Input component on your Worksheet:

■ Drag the **1.0** icon from the Component Palettes to your Work-sheet. The Input component appears.

■ You can type values into the cells, import values from a data file, or paste them in from the Clipboard.

Once you've done so, the Input component might look like this:

12.50	125.00
15.74	354.00
18.50	220.00
20.00	150.00

Typing in values

To enter values into the Input component:

■ Double-click the component.

- If necessary, you can show more cells by clicking on one of the handles, holding the mouse button down, and dragging out.

- Enter values into the cells. Pressing [**Enter**] will bring you to the next cell down. You can enter any kind of decimal or e-format number such as 3.4 or 2i or 4e-6.

Tip   If you don't double-click the component before using the handles to enlarge the component, you'll simply stretch the component rather than enlarge the view.

If you type any imaginary or complex values, all the values in the component are displayed as complex values. For example, if you type **4** in one cell and **6i** in another cell, the values will display as **4.00+0.00i** and **0.00+6.00i**.

Importing values from a data file

To import data from an external data file after placing the Input component on a Worksheet:

- Click the component with the right mouse button.

- Choose **Import** from the pop-up menu. The Read from File dialog box appears.

- In the "Files of Type" text box, choose the type of file from which you want to import data.

- Use the dialog box to browse to the data file and click "Open."

Note   You can choose to import the following types of files, among others: ASCII text, MATLAB, Excel, Lotus 1-2-3, Quattro Pro, dBase III, and S-PLUS.

Pasting in data from the Clipboard

If your data is stored in another application, but not in a saved file, you can copy it to the Clipboard and paste it into the Input component. To do so:

- Select the data in the other application and copy it to the Clipboard. In most applications, you do this by choosing **Copy** from the **Edit** menu.

- Place the Input component on a MathConnex Worksheet.

- Click it with the right mouse button so that a pop-up menu appears.

- Choose **Paste Table** from the pop-up menu.

Controlling the format of the values in the Input component

To control the way the numbers in the Input Component are displayed:

- Click the component to select it.

- Click the component with the right mouse button so that you see the pop-up menu.

- Choose **Properties** from the pop-up menu.

- Click the Format tab.

- Enter the settings you want and click "OK."

The settings on the Format page are as follows:

Displayed Precision: Choose or type an integer n. Determines the number of values to the right of the decimal place.

Show trailing zeros: Check this box to make all displayed results have as many digits to the right of the decimal point as required by the current choice of Displayed Precision.

Exponential Threshold: Choose or type an integer n. Values smaller than 10^{-n} or greater than 10^n are displayed in exponential notation.

Complex Threshold: Choose or type an integer n. If the ratio between the real and imaginary part of a complex number is less than 10^n or greater than 10^{-n}, then the smaller part is not shown.

Zero Threshold: Choose or type an integer n. Values smaller than 10^{-n} are displayed as zero.

Show row/column labels: Check this box to display the row and column numbers associated with the values in the table.

Click "Font" to modify the font used to display numbers in the Input component.

Note These display settings only affect the appearance of numbers in the Input component. They do not affect the precision of values sent from the component as output. The values are always sent using the maximum values for each setting.

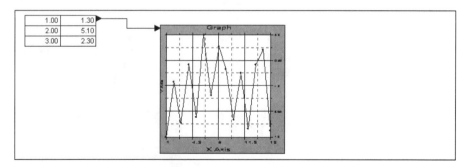

Figure 4-1: The Input component provides data for a system.

Editing the Input component

Once you've imported or typed values into the Input component, you can edit them. First, double-click the component to activate it and then click on whichever cells you want to edit.

To delete a row or column of cells:

- Double-click the Input component to activate it.

- Click in a cell in the row or column to delete.

- Click the cell with the right mouse button to display a pop-up menu.

- Choose **Delete Cells** to bring up the Delete dialog box.

- Click either Entire Row or Entire Column and click "OK."

To insert a row or column of cells:

- Double-click the Input component to activate it.

- Click in a cell in the row to the left of where the new row or column will be inserted.

- Click the cell with the right mouse button to display a pop-up menu.

- Choose **Insert Cells** to bring up the Insert dialog box.

- Click either Row or Column and click "OK."

File Read/Write

Using the File Read/Write component you can:

- Establish a live connection to a data file.

- Read data from the file or write data to it.

To place the File Read/Write component on your Worksheet:

- Drag the [icon] icon from the Component Palettes to your Worksheet to launch the Setup Wizard.

- Choose "Read from data source" if you want to read in data from a file. Choose "Write to a data source" to write to a data file.

- Press "Next" to go to the second page of the Wizard, shown at right.

- From the drop-down list in the File Source box, choose the type of data file you want to read from or write to.

- Type the path to the data file you want to read or click "Browse" to locate it.

- Press "Finish."

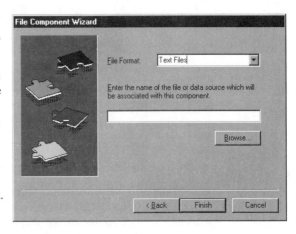

You'll see the File Read/Write component and the path to the data file. For example, if you read from a data file called DATA.TXT, you'll see:

Note   You can choose to read from or write to the following types of files, among others: ASCII text, MATLAB, Excel, Lotus 1-2-3, Quattro Pro, dBase III, and S-PLUS.

When you run a system containing the File Read/Write component, data are read in from or written to the data file every time the component is triggered. When the File Read/Write component writes to a file, any data already existing in the file are overwritten. If you don't want existing data to be overwritten, click the component with the right mouse button and choose **Overwrite File** from the pop-up menu. Then when the component is triggered, you will be prompted whether to overwrite existing data.

When the File Read/Write component is reading from a file, it reads in the entire data file. To read in only certain rows or columns of a data file:

■ Click the component with the right mouse button so that you see the pop-up menu.

■ Choose **Properties** from the pop-up menu to bring up the Properties dialog box.

■ Click the File Options tab and specify the row and columns at which to start and stop reading.

To change the data file or type that's being read from or written to:

■ Click with the right mouse button on the component and select **Choose File** from the component pop-up menu.

■ In the "Files of type" text box, choose a type of file. Use the dialog box to browse to the data file, select the data file, and click "Open."

Ramp

Use the Ramp component to generate a series of real scalar values and pass them into a system. This component is useful for problems requiring iteration or incremental data.

To insert the Ramp component in a Worksheet:

■ Drag the icon from the Component Palettes to your Worksheet. The Ramp component appears.

■ Click the component with the right mouse button and choose **Properties** from the pop-up menu.

■ Click the Ramp tab and specify the starting value and the increment/step value.

When you connect the output port of the Ramp component to another component and run the system, the Ramp component generates one value at a time. The attached component receives each value as it is produced. If one value isn't passed further along the system or if the attached component can't accept more than one value, the Ramp won't generate another value.

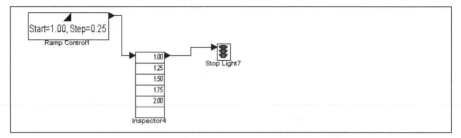

Figure 4-2: The Ramp component generates values. Here, several values accumulate in the Inspector component (see page 49).

Global Variable

To use the output from one component in another, you must connect the two components. If you want to send a single output to several different components, you must therefore connect the one component to several different components. This can involve a lot of wires and give a messy appearance to a MathConnex system.

An alternative to several connections and wires is to use the Global Variable component. The Global Variable component lets you give a name to the output from a component and refer to it without having to make a connection to the component producing it.

To give a name to some data using the Global Variable component:

■ Drag the ![icon] icon from the Component Palettes to your Work-sheet. The Global Variable component appears.

■ Click the component with the right mouse button and choose **Properties** from the pop-up menu.

■ Click the Variable Name tab and enter a name for the data. Make sure that "This component sets the value" is checked.

■ Connect the output port from the component generating the data to tag to the input port of the Global Variable.

When the system runs, the data going into the Global Variable are tagged with the name you specified.

To refer to that data with its name via the Global Variable component:

■ Place a Global Variable component on the Worksheet. By default, it has the same variable name as the one you created previously.

■ Connect the output port from the Global Variable component to another component.

If you want to create a new Global Variable, follow the steps above but replace the name in the Variable Name tab with a new name and check "This component sets the value."

When a Global Variable component receives values as input, all other Global Variable components with the same variable name send those values as output. To see this

behavior, choose **Highlight Components** from the **Run** menu and press ![button] repeatedly.

The example below shows how one instance of a Global Variable gives a name to some output, and other instances refer to that output.

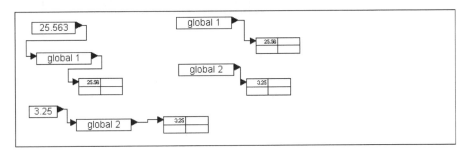

Figure 4-3: The names "Global 1" and "Global 2" are given to some data via the Global Variable component. Other instances of the Global Variable components with these names refer to the data.

Components for viewing results

As data travels from component to component along a wire in a MathConnex system, you can see what the data is at a certain point by either looking at it in a table or in a graph. To look at the data in a table, use the Inspector component. To visualize the data in a two- or three-dimensional graph, use the Graph component or the 3D graph component. If you have MathSoft's Axum or S-PLUS installed, you can also create 2D and 3D graphs using components based on these applications.

Inspector

Using the Inspector component you can:

- Display the value of data on a wire in a spreadsheet format.

- Export the data being displayed to a data file.

- Accumulate data as it flows through a system.

To insert the Inspector component to the Worksheet:

- Drag the icon from the Component Palettes to your Work-sheet. The Inspector component appears with a single input port.

When you connect the output port of another component to the Inspector component and run the system, the Inspector component displays the input and sends it along as output.

To see more values in the Inspector, double-click it. You will see scrollbars that allow you to scroll through the Inspector. You will also see handles along the edges of the Inspector. To resize the table, move the cursor to one of these handles so that it changes to a double-headed arrow, press and hold down the mouse button, and drag the cursor in the direction you want the table's dimensions to change.

Tip   If you don't double-click the component before using the handles to enlarge the component, you'll simply stretch the component rather than enlarge the view.

Adding output ports

By default, the Inspector component has one input port and no output ports. If you want to send output from the Inspector component, however, you can add a single output port. To do so:

- Click the component with the right mouse button to bring up the pop-up menu.

- Choose **Add Output Port**.

If you want to remove the output port later, choose **Remove Output Port** from the pop-up menu.

Controlling the format of the values in the Inspector

To control the way the numbers in the Inspector are displayed:

- Click the component with the right mouse button so that you see the pop-up menu.

- Choose **Properties** from the pop-up menu.

- Click the Format tab to show the page at right.

- Enter the settings you want and click "OK."

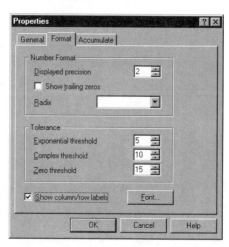

The settings on the Format page are as follows:

Displayed Precision: Choose or type an integer n. Determines the number of values to the right of the decimal place.

Show trailing zeros: Check this box to make all displayed results have as many digits to the right of the decimal point as required by the current choice of Displayed Precision.

Exponential Threshold: Choose or type an integer n. Values smaller than 10^{-n} or greater than 10^n are displayed in exponential notation.

Complex Threshold: Choose or type an integer n. If the ratio between the real and imaginary part of a complex number is less than 10^n or greater than 10^{-n}, then the smaller part is not shown.

Zero Threshold: Choose or type an integer n. Values smaller than 10^{-n} are displayed as zero.

Show row/column labels: Check this box to display the row and column numbers associated with the values in the table.

Click "Font" to modify the font used to display numbers in the Input component.

Note   These display settings only affect the appearance of numbers in the Inspector component. They do not affect the values sent from the component as output. The values are always sent using the maximum values for each setting.

Exporting to a data file

You can export the values you see in the Inspector to a data file. To do so:

■ Click the Inspector component with the right mouse button so that you see the component's pop-up menu.

■ Choose **Export**. You will see the Write to File dialog box.

■ In the "Files of type" text box, select the format of the file you'd like to create. Use the dialog box to browse to the folder in which the data file will be created and enter the name of the data file you wish to create. Then click "Open."

Note   You can choose to export data to the following types of files, among others: formatted text, tab-delimited text, comma-separated values, MATLAB, Excel, Lotus 1-2-3, Quattro Pro, dBase III, and S-PLUS.

Accumulating data

The Inspector is also useful for storing data as it flows through the system. For example, you might want to run a system 15 times, capturing a value from each run. Then, once you've gathered 15 values, you want to send them further along the system. To gather values this way:

- Click the Inspector component with the right mouse button.

- Choose **Properties** from the pop-up menu.

- Click the Accumulate tab.

- Check Accumulate Data.

- Specify the total number of rows and columns of data values you'd like to accumulate and whether the values should accumulate row by row or column by column.

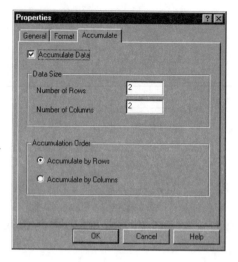

When the Inspector is configured to accumulate data, it has one input port and one output port. It accumulates the number of values you specified in terms of rows and columns and then sends the values along the wire connected to the output port.

Figure 4-2 on page 48 shows an example in which the Inspector component is set to accumulate 5 rows and 1 column of data generated from the Ramp component.

Graph

The Graph component allows you to create a two-dimensional graph in a system. It accepts one or more pairs of *x*- and *y*-coordinates as input and graphs them.

To place the Graph component on your Worksheet:

- Drag the 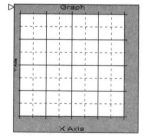 icon from the Component Palettes to your Worksheet. The Graph component appears with a single input port by default, but the component can accommodate up to four inputs and an equal number of outputs. See "Adding and removing ports" on page 25 to find out how to add or remove ports.

- Connect the output port of a component that is outputting coordinate pairs to the input port of the Graph component.

When you run the system, the Graph component creates a graph. This allows you to graph a group of data points or one data point at a time if the data are being passed as single values through the system.

Note The data passed to the Graph component must be stored in $n \times 2$ form, where each of the rows contains an ordered pair (x, y). See Figure 4-4 for an example.

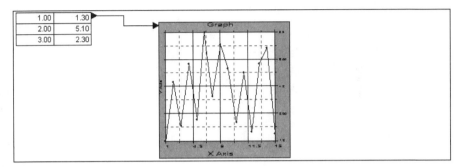

Figure 4-4: The Graph component graphs rows containing (x, y) coordinates.

Modifying graph properties

To control specifics about the graph such as which input values to graph and whether there are labels or tick marks:

■ Click the component with the right mouse button.

■ Choose **Properties** from the pop-up menu.

Use the Plot, Labels, and Axes pages to control the appearance of the graph:

■ Use the **Plot** page to control data history (how often to reset the graph), colors, and style settings such as line and symbol types.

■ Use the **Labels** page to specify the axis labels, title, and legend used on the graph.

■ Use the **Axes** page to control whether the Axes are boxed or crossed in the lower right corner and to specify scales, ranges, and whether tick marks or grid lines appear.

Note To make changes in the **Axes** page for either the *x*- or *y*-axis, choose either x-axis or y-axis in the "Assign Settings For" box.

For more information on the various options in each tabbed page of the Properties dialog box, click "Help" in the dialog box.

Tip   You can save your customized graph settings by saving the custom graph as a module. Fonts and graph characteristics are stored in the module and can be easily dropped into other Worksheets. See page 17 for more information about modules.

Copying the Graph component

To copy a Graph component to the Clipboard:

■ Click the component with the right mouse button to display the component's pop-up menu.

■ Click **Copy to the Clipboard** in the pop-up menu.

The graph is copied to the Clipboard as an enhanced metafile. When you open another application that supports the enhanced metafile format (EMF), you can paste the copied graph into that application.

3D Graph

The 3D Graph component allows you to create three-dimensional graphs of data that are run through your system. Based on the OpenGL graphics engine and supporting sophisticated formatting and lighting options, the 3D Graph component can render surface plots, parametric surface plots, contour plots, 3D scatter plots, 3D bar plots, and vector field plots identical to those created by Mathcad 8 Professional.

To place the 3D Graph component onto the Worksheet:

■ Drag the ![icon] icon from the Component Palettes to your Worksheet. The 3D Graph component appears with axes and with a single input port by default.

■ Connect the output port of a component that is outputting a matrix to the input port of the 3D Graph component.

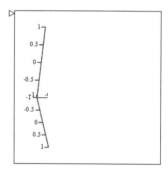

When you run the system, the 3D Graph component creates a graph based on data that are output from the component connected to its input port. See Figure 4-5 for an example. By default you see a surface plot, but you can convert the graph to another type, as follows:

■ Click the component with the right mouse button to bring up the pop-up menu.

■ Choose **Properties**.

■ Click a plot type in the Display As section of the General page.

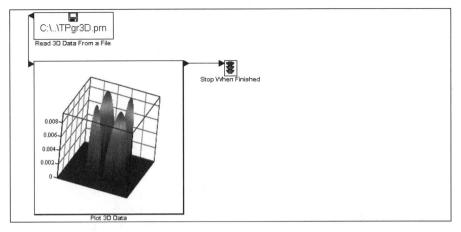

Figure 4-5: Displaying data in the 3D Graph component.

Adding input and output ports

By default, the 3D Graph component has one input port and no output ports. Most of the graphs that can be rendered by the 3D Graph component require a single matrix input, but some require three matrix or vector inputs (see table below). To change the number of input ports from one to three:

■ Click the component with the right mouse button to bring up the pop-up menu.

■ Choose **Three Inputs**.

To revert to a single input port, choose **One Input** from the pop-up menu.

A 3D Graph component can have as many output ports as it has input ports. To add output ports to your component:

■ Click the component with the right mouse button to bring up the pop-up menu.

■ Choose **Outputs**.

Inputs required for 3D graph types

The following table indicates the number of inputs required for each kind of 3D graph.

3D plot	Inputs
`Surface plot`	One input matrix whose row and column numbers represent the x- and y-axis values. The matrix elements themselves are the z-values.
`Parametric surface plot`	Three input matrices containing, respectively, the x-, y-, and z-coordinates of points on the surface.
`Contour plot`	One input matrix whose row and column numbers represent the x- and y-axis values. The matrix elements themselves are the z-values.
`3D scatter plot`	Three input vectors containing, respectively, the x-, y-, and z-coordinates of points in space.

3D bar plot	A matrix whose row and column numbers represent the *x*- and *y*-axis values. The matrix elements themselves are the *z*-values, or the heights of the bars.
Vector field plot	A single input matrix of complex values whose row and column numbers represent the vector *x*- and *y*-coordinates. The real part of each matrix element is the *x*-component of a vector. The imaginary part of each element is the *y*-component of a vector.

Modifying 3D graph properties

Once you insert a 3D graph using the 3D Graph component, you can use a variety of formatting and lighting options to control the way the graph appears.

Tip For an overview of the formatting capabilities available for Open GL–based 3D graphs, see the *Mathcad 8 User's Guide* and the Mathcad on-line Help.

In general, to format the graph:

■ Click the component with the right mouse button to bring up the pop-up menu.

■ Choose **Properties**.

■ Use the options on the pages in the dialog box to format the graph. Click on a tab to go to a particular page.

Some options available on certain pages in the dialog box depend on the kind of graph you are formatting. Options on other pages are available for any 3D graph:

■ The **General** page gives you access to basic options that control the overall appearance of the graph. Use these options to control the position of a graph, set the axis style, draw a border or a box, or convert one 3D graph to another type.

■ The options on the **Axes** page allow you to control exactly how each axis looks. You can specify the weight of each axis and whether it has numbers or tick marks. You can also specify the axis limits. Use the tabs at the top of the page to format the *x*-, *y*-, or *z*-axis.

■ The **Backplanes** page has options for specifying whether a backplane is filled with a color, has a border, or has grid lines or tick marks. Use the tabs at the top of the page to format the *x*-*y*, *y*-*z*, or *x*-*z* backplane.

■ Use the options on the **Appearance** page to format the surfaces, lines, and points that make up a graph. For example, the options here let you apply color directly to a graph's surface, its contours, or its lines and points.

■ The **Lighting** page options control both the overall lighting of the graph as well as individual lights directed onto it.

- The **Title** page gives you a text box for entering a title for the graph and options for specifying the location of the title on the graph.

- The options on the **Special** page are for controlling graph characteristics related to specific kinds of graphs. For example, the Bar Plot Layout options let you specify the way the bars are arranged in a 3D bar plot.

- The **Advanced** page has options which you are likely to use only when you need very fine control over the appearance of a graph, such as the vertical scale.

For details on the options available on a particular page in the formatting dialog box, click "Help" at the bottom of the dialog box.

Rotating a 3D graph

You can rotate a 3D graph interactively with the mouse or by specifying parameters in the Properties dialog box.

To rotate a three-dimensional graph interactively by using the mouse:

- Click in the graph, and hold the mouse button down.

- Drag the mouse in the direction you want the graph to turn.

- Release the mouse button when the graph is in the desired position.

To rotate a three-dimensional graph by using the Properties dialog box:

- Click the component with the right mouse button to bring up the pop-up menu.

- Choose **Properties**.

- Click the General tab.

- Edit the settings for Rotation, Tilt, and Twist in the View options.

- Click "Apply" to preview the graph. Click "OK" to close the dialog box.

Spinning a 3D graph

You can set a 3D graph in motion so that it spins continuously about an axis of rotation:

- Click in the graph, and hold the [**Shift**] key and the mouse button down.

- Drag the mouse in the direction you want the graph to spin.

- Release the mouse button to set the graph in motion.

The graph spins continuously until you click again inside the graph.

Zooming a 3D graph

You can zoom in or out of a 3D graph interactively or by specifying a zoom factor in the Properties dialog box.

To zoom in on a three-dimensional graph by using the mouse:

- Click in the graph, and hold the [**Ctrl**] key and the mouse button down.

- Drag the mouse toward the top of the graph to zoom out, or drag the mouse toward the bottom to zoom in.

- Release the mouse button when the graph is at the desired zoom factor.

Tip   If you use an IntelliMouse-compatible mouse with a center wheel, you can rotate the wheel to zoom in or out of a three-dimensional graph.

To zoom in or out of a three-dimensional graph by using the Properties dialog box:

- Click the component with the right mouse button to bring up the pop-up menu.

- Choose **Properties**.

- Click the General tab.

- Edit the Zoom setting in the View options.

- Click "Apply" to preview the graph. Click "OK" to close the dialog box.

Axum

Axum is a technical graphing and data analysis application available from MathSoft, and the Axum component gives you access to a variety of two and three-dimensional graph types in that application. To use the component, you must have Axum 5.0c installed (but not necessarily running) on your system.

Using the Axum component you can:

- Create over 75 different types of 2D and 3D graphs.

- Double-click the Axum component to activate Axum to format every detail of your graph.

Tip   When an Axum component is activated, Axum runs in the background. You therefore need enough available memory to run Axum and MathConnex simultaneously.

To place an Axum component on your Worksheet:

- Drag the [icon] icon from the Component Palettes to your Worksheet to launch the Axum Setup Wizard.

- Choose the type of graph you would like to insert and click "Next."

- Choose a plot type. The available choices depend on the type of graph you selected.

- Click "Finish."

An Axum graph of the type you specified is inserted into your Worksheet with an appropriate number of input ports. There are no output ports because the Axum component does not send output.

When you connect a component to the Axum component and run the system, the input data is plotted. See Figure 4-6 for an example.

Note The form of the data you pass into the Axum component depends on the kind of graph you want to create. See the *Axum User's Guide* or on-line Help to find out the form in which to provide the data for a given plot type.

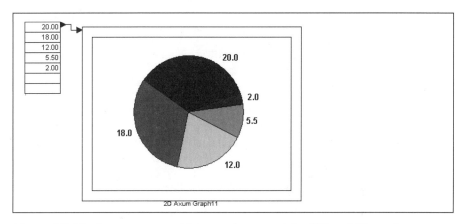

Figure 4-6: The Axum component lets you place a variety of 2D and 3D graphs in a MathConnex system.

Editing the Axum component

You can change the format of a graph that you created using the Axum component using Axum features. For example, you can change the colors in the graph, the labeling, whether there are grid lines, etc.

To edit the Axum component:

■ Double-click the Axum component in your Worksheet to activate Axum. The menus and toolbars in MathConnex will change to Axum's menu and toolbars.

■ Format the graph using Axum commands and features. See the *Axum User's Guide* or on-line Help for more information on editing graphs.

Tip If an Axum component is displayed as an icon and you double-click it, the menus and toolbars in MathConnex won't change to Axum's, but a separate Axum window appears.

S-PLUS Graph

S-PLUS is a sophisticated exploratory data analysis and statistical application available from MathSoft. The S-PLUS Graph component is an embedded S-PLUS graph sheet that allows you to integrate a wide range of two- and three-dimensional graphs, including Trellis plots, into your MathConnex systems. You must have S-PLUS 4.5 or higher installed on your computer (but not necessarily running) to use this component.

To insert an S-PLUS Graph component:

- Drag the ▨ icon from the Component Palettes to your Worksheet. The S-PLUS Graph component appears with a single input port by default, but the component can accommodate up to four inputs and four outputs. See "Adding and removing ports" on page 25 to find out how to add or remove ports.

> **S-PLUS**
> **Graph**

- Connect the output port of a component that is outputting a matrix to the input port of the S-PLUS Graph component.

When you run the system, the S-PLUS Graph component creates a graph based on data that are output from the component connected to its input port. The only way to send meaningful values out of the output ports is to set the graph type to "Call Graph Script" (see below) and specify the outputs within the script.

Note By default, the data on the input ports are sent into S-PLUS variables named `in0`, `in1`, `in2`, and so on. The S-PLUS variables `out0`, `out1`, `out2`, and so on define the data to be passed from the output ports. To change these names, choose **Properties** from the component's pop-up menu, and enter new names in the Input Variables and Output Variables pages.

Types of graphs

To access the different graph types for the component:

- Click with the right mouse button on the component.

- Choose **Properties** from the pop-up menu.

The Graph Type page in the Properties dialog box allows you to select one of the following:

- **Line Plot**. This default graph type shows one to four traces on a single graph. Each input is interpreted as a matrix with either one column (interpreted as y-values to plot against $x = 1 \ldots n$), or two columns (interpreted as x- and y-values).

- **Gui Graph**. This graph type supports any of the S-PLUS graphs available through the S-PLUS graphical user interface. For this component, the inputs are interpreted as arrays whose data columns are passed to the graph-creation routines. The graph type rendered is specified in the "Axis Type" and "Plot Type" fields. Click "Choose

Axis/Plot Type" to open the S-PLUS dialog box for choosing plot types and viewing thumbnail images of the different types.

Note On Gui graphs, particular inputs can be treated as conditioning variables in order to produce Trellis plots (conditioned, multipanel plots). To do this, click the checkboxes in the Input Variables page of the Properties dialog box.

■ **Call Graph Script**. This graph type supports any commands that generate "traditional" (version 3.3-style) S-PLUS graphics. To enter commands, open the Script Editor by choosing **Edit Script** from the component's pop-up menu. The script you enter can contain any S-PLUS code, with calls to `plot()`, `points()`, etc. to generate one or more graphs. The inputs and outputs and static variables are specified on the Input Variables and Output Variables tabs of the Properties dialog box, just as they are in the S-PLUS Script component (see below). If the script is totally empty, by default the script is defined as `plot(in0)`. The variable `graphsheet.name` can be accessed within the script to get the name of the graph sheet. When you are finished editing the script, choose **Close & Return** from the Script Editor's **File** menu or press [**Esc**].

Note Normally, the plot is cleared before each call to the script to update the graph. If "Clear plot before each call" is unchecked on the Graph Type page of the Properties dialog box, this is not done. In this way you can collect multiple plots in different pages.

Computational components

While some components introduce data into a system or display it in a table or graph, the following components let you manipulate the data mathematically or in any other ways allowed by the component:

■ Mathcad component

■ S-PLUS Script component

■ Excel component

■ MATLAB component

■ ConnexScript component

For example, you might use Mathcad to perform linear regression on a set of data, or you might use the Excel component to exchange rows and columns of values.

Note To use the Mathcad, S-PLUS Script, Excel, or MATLAB component, you must have the corresponding application installed, but not necessarily running, on your system. When a Mathcad, S-PLUS Script, Excel, or MATLAB component is activated, the corresponding application runs in the background. You therefore need enough available memory to run both the application and MathConnex simultaneously. Note also that while a component such as the Mathcad or Excel component may be derived from an existing file, it is an object and cannot change the content of that file.

Mathcad

MathSoft's Mathcad is an integrated environment for performing, documenting, and communicating technical calculations. The Mathcad component lets you create or connect to a Mathcad worksheet and pass numerical data between a MathConnex system and a Mathcad worksheet.

When using the Mathcad component you can:

■ Manipulate data using Mathcad functions and operators.

■ Use a Mathcad worksheet as a data source for introducing data into a system.

■ Apply a Mathcad worksheet iteratively in a computational process.

To use the component, you must have Mathcad 8 Professional installed (but not necessarily running) on your system.

To place the Mathcad component on your Worksheet:

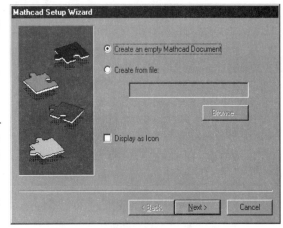

■ Drag the icon from the Component Palettes to your Worksheet. This launches the Mathcad Setup Wizard.

■ To connect to an existing Mathcad file, choose "Create from file," and type the path name in the text box or use the Browse button to locate the file; then click "Open." If you don't want to connect to a previously created file, choose "Create an empty Mathcad worksheet."

■ Check Display as Icon if you want to display the Mathcad component as an icon in the Worksheet rather than as a window onto a Mathcad worksheet.

Although you won't see the Mathcad equations in the component when you display it as an icon, you can double-click the component to edit it, and a separate, moderately sized window appears. If you don't display the component as an icon, you must resize the component inside MathConnex in order to get a reasonably sized window in which to work.

- When you click "Next," the Wizard brings you to the next page where you will specify the number of inputs and outputs.

- When you click "Finish," the Mathcad component appears in your Worksheet with the appropriate number of input and output ports. For example, a Mathcad component with one input and two output ports would look like this:

If you chose to create a new worksheet, you should enter equations and calculations into it by doing the following:

- Double-click the Mathcad component in the Worksheet to activate it. The Mathcad component opens. The menus and toolbars change to Mathcad menus and toolbars.

If the Mathcad component is instead displayed as an icon, a separate Mathcad window opens when you double-click.

- Type in the Mathcad component worksheet just as you would in a regular Mathcad worksheet: enter equations, define functions, create graphs, etc. Use the variable names **in0**, **in1**, etc. to refer to the inputs. Each input can be a scalar, vector, or matrix.

- Define variables **out0**, **out1**, etc. if there will be output from the component. The values of these variables will be sent out of the Mathcad component to the next component in the system.

To enlarge the Mathcad component, first double-click it to activate it. You'll see handles along the sides of the component. Move the cursor to one of these handles so that it changes to a double-headed arrow. Press and hold down the mouse button and drag the cursor in the direction you want the component's dimensions to change.

When you connect the Mathcad component into a MathConnex system and run the system, the input data flows into the Mathcad component worksheet and is assigned to the Mathcad variables **in0**, **in1**, etc. The values in **out0**, **out1**, etc. flow out of the component.

Editing the Mathcad component

Once you set up a Mathcad component, you can add or remove inputs or outputs. To do so:

- Click the component with the right mouse button to bring up the pop-up menu.

- Choose **Add Input Port**, **Remove Input Port**, **Add Output Port**, or **Remove Output Port**.

To make changes to the equations, graphs, etc. in the Mathcad component, double-click it to activate it and make the necessary changes.

S-PLUS Script

MathSoft's S-PLUS is a sophisticated data analysis environment and statistical application based on the S language. The S-PLUS Script component allows you to write and execute S-PLUS programs and link them to other computations in your MathConnex Worksheet. To use this component, you must have S-PLUS 4.5 or higher installed (but not necessarily running) on your system.

When using the S-PLUS Script component, you can:

- Manipulate data using S-PLUS functions.

- Use a S-PLUS file as a data source for a system.

To place the S-PLUS Script component on your Worksheet:

- Drag the ▨ icon from the Component Palettes to your Worksheet. The S-PLUS Script component appears in your Worksheet. By default, the S-PLUS Script component has one input port and one output port, but the component can accommodate up to four inputs and four outputs. See "Adding and removing ports" on page 25 to find out how to add or remove ports.

- Double-click the S-PLUS Script component in the Worksheet. The S-PLUS Script component opens a script editing window.

- Type in the S-PLUS Script component worksheet just as you would in a regular S-PLUS file. Use the variable names **in0**, **in1**, etc. to refer to the inputs. Each input can be a scalar, vector, or two-dimensional matrix. If there is output from the component, define variables **out0**, **out1**, etc. The values of these variables are sent out of the S-PLUS Script component to the next component(s) in the system.

- Choose **Apply Changes** from the **File** menu or click ☑.

- Choose **Close and Return** from the **File** menu or press [**Esc**].

Tip Clicking ☑ runs the script so that you can see any errors while the Script Editor window is open.

When you connect the S-PLUS Script component into a system and run the system, the input data flow into the S-PLUS Script component worksheet as **in0**, **in1**, etc. The values in **out0**, **out1**, etc. flow out of the component. To edit the S-PLUS Script component, double-click it to activate it and make the necessary changes.

Note To use names other than **in0**, **in1**, etc. and **out0**, **out1**, etc., click the component with the right mouse button and choose **Properties** from the pop-up menu. Use the Input Variables page to change the input names. Use the Output Variables page to change the Output names.

Script syntax

Your S-PLUS code, which can include multiple statements, is inserted within an automatically created function to run the component. This code can use temporary variables, but any temporary variables are not visible outside of the component (unless **assign** is called to change the S-PLUS databases). For example, a script could contain **out0<-sin(in0)** to set the output to the sine of the input.

Tip To declare static variables, which keep their values between calls to the script, add the variable names (separated by commas) to the Static Variable Names field on the Input Variables page of the component's Properties dialog box. All static variables are reset whenever the script itself is changed, however.

The following variables can be accessed within a script:

■ **input.var.names** and **output.var.names** are vectors of strings that give the input and output variable names for the component. You can use these variables to write scripts that handle different numbers of inputs and outputs.

■ **first.call** has a value of T if this is the first time this script has been executed. This variable can be used to initialize static variables.

Note If **Show Captured Results** on the S-PLUS Script component's pop-up menu is checked, the component displays the text produced by the last execution of the S-PLUS program, including any printing done by the script, as if it had been executed at the S-PLUS command line. Capturing this text can slow down the execution. Error messages are always captured, however, so after an error occurs the display can be switched to see the error message.

Importing and exporting text in the S-PLUS Script component

You can import text from other files to the Script Editor and export text from the Script Editor to other files. The source file types recognized include S-PLUS, ConnexScript, and ASCII text.

To import the contents of another file into the Script Editor:

■ Position the cursor at the line where you want to import code.

■ Choose **Import** from the **File** menu, and browse to locate the file you want to import.

■ Click "Open."

To export the contents of the Script Editor to another file:

■ Choose **Export** from the **File** menu, and specify the path and filename of the target file.

■ Select the desired file type.

■ Click "Save."

The entire contents of the Script Editor window is exported to the target file.

Excel

The Excel component lets you:

■ Use an Microsoft Excel worksheet as a data source for introducing data into a system.

■ Manipulate data using Excel functions and operators.

■ Display data in an Excel worksheet.

To use this component, you must have Excel for Windows 95 version 7.0 or higher installed (but not necessarily running) on your system.

To place the Excel component on your Worksheet:

■ Drag the icon from the Component Palettes to your Worksheet. This launches the Excel Setup Wizard.

■ To connect to an existing Excel file, choose "Create from file," and type the path name in the text box or use the Browse button to locate the file; then click "Open." If you don't want to connect to a previously created file, choose "Create an empty Excel Worksheet."

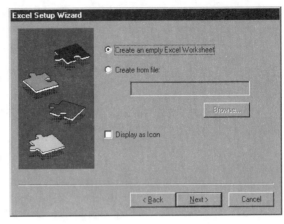

■ Check Display as Icon if you want to display the component as an icon rather than as a window onto an Excel file.

Tip Although you won't see the Excel worksheet in the component when you display it as an icon, you can double-click it to edit it, and a separate, moderately sized window appears. If you don't display the component as an icon, you must resize the component inside MathConnex in order to get a reasonably sized window in which to work.

■ Click "Next" to specify:

The number of inputs and outputs: choose a number between 0 and 4 for each.

Input ranges: the Excel cells in which the values of each input will be stored. Enter the starting cell, which is the cell that will hold the element in the upper left corner of an array of values. For example, for an input variable containing a 3×3 matrix of values, you can specify A1 as the starting cell, and the values will be placed in the cells A1 through C3.

Output ranges: the Excel cells whose values will be sent as output. For example, enter C2:L11 to output the values in cells C2 through L11.

■ Click "Finish."

You'll see the Excel component in your Worksheet with the appropriate number of input and output ports. For example, an Excel component that has no inputs but provides two sets of output would look like this:

If you created an empty Excel worksheet or if you want to manipulate the data using Excel, double-click the Excel component. The Excel component opens and the Math-Connex menus and toolbars change to those of Excel.

Figure 4-7 shows an example of an Excel component introducing data to a system.

Note If the Excel component is displayed as an icon, a separate Excel window opens when you double-click the component.

When you connect the Excel component into a system and run the system, the input data flows into the Excel component in the cells you specified in the Wizard. The output values will be gathered from the cells you specified and flow out of the component.

Tip To see more or fewer rows and columns, double-click the Excel component to activate it. You'll see handles along the sides of the component. Move the cursor to one of these handles so that it changes to a double-headed arrow. Press and hold down the mouse button and drag the cursor in the direction you want the component's dimensions to change.

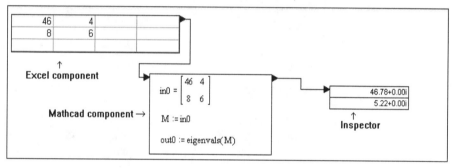

Figure 4-7: Passing data from an Excel component to a Mathcad component.

Making changes to the inputs and outputs

Once you set up an Excel component, you can add or remove input or output variables, or you can change the cell ranges for inputs and outputs you initially specified in the Setup Wizard. To do so:

■ Click the component with the right mouse button to bring up the pop-up menu.

■ Choose **Add Input Port, Remove Input Port, Add Output Port,** or **Remove Output Port**.

When you add input or output ports or wish to reconfigure existing ports, you'll need to specify which cells in the component store the input(s) and which provide the output(s). To do so:

■ Click the component with the right mouse button to bring up the pop-up menu.

- Choose **Properties** from the pop-up menu.

- Click either the Inputs tab or the Outputs tab and specify a range of cells for each input and each output.

MATLAB

The MATLAB component lets you connect to the MATLAB environment and pass numerical data between a MathConnex system and MATLAB variables. To use this component, you must have MATLAB 4.2c or higher installed (but not necessarily running) on your system.

When using the MATLAB component, you can:

- Manipulate data using MATLAB functions.

- Use a MATLAB file as a data source for a system.

- Use MATLAB graphics functions to display data.

To place the MATLAB component on your Worksheet:

- Drag the .m icon from the Component Palettes to your Worksheet. The MATLAB component appears in your Worksheet. By default, the MATLAB component has one input port and one output port, but the component can accommodate up to four inputs and four outputs. See "Adding and removing ports" on page 25 to find out how to add or remove ports.

- Double-click the MATLAB component in the Worksheet. The MATLAB component opens as a text editing window.

- Type in the MATLAB component worksheet just as you would in a regular MATLAB file. Use the variable names **in0**, **in1**, etc. to refer to the inputs. Each input can be a scalar, vector, or two-dimensional matrix. If there will be output from the component, define variables **out0**, **out1**, etc. The values of these variables are sent out of the MATLAB component to the next component in the system.

- Choose **Apply Changes** from the **File** menu or click ☑.

- Choose **Close and Return** from the **File** menu or press [**Esc**].

Tip   Clicking ☑ runs the script so that you can see any errors while the Script Editor window is open.

When you connect the MATLAB component into a system and run the system, the input data flow into the MATLAB component worksheet as **in0**, **in1**, etc. The values in **out0**, **out1**, etc. flow out of the component. To edit the MATLAB component, double-click it to activate it and make the necessary changes.

Importing and exporting text in the MATLAB component

You can import text from other files to the Script Editor and export text from the Script Editor to other files. The source file types recognized include MATLAB, ConnexScript, and ASCII text.

To import the contents of another file into the Script Editor:

- Position the cursor at the line where you want to import code.

- Choose **Import** from the **File** menu, and browse to locate the file you want to import.

- Click "Open."

To export the contents of the Script Editor to another file:

- Choose **Export** from the **File** menu, and specify the path and filename of the target file.

- Select the desired file type.

- Click "Save."

The entire contents of the Script Editor window is exported to the target file.

ConnexScript

You can use the ConnexScript component for short, straightforward calculations using the ConnexScript language and its built-in functions.

To place the ConnexScript component on your Worksheet:

- Drag the ▣ icon from the Component Palettes onto the Worksheet. The ConnexScript component appears as an icon with one input port and one output port by default, but the component can accommodate up to four inputs and four outputs. See "Adding and removing ports" on page 25 to find out how to add or remove ports.

- Double-click the component to bring up the Script Editor:

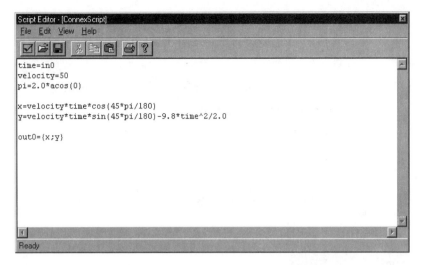

```
Script Editor - [ConnexScript]
File  Edit  View  Help

time=in0
velocity=50
pi=2.0*acos(0)

x=velocity*time*cos(45*pi/180)
y=velocity*time*sin(45*pi/180)-9.8*time^2/2.0

out0={x;y}

Ready
```

- Enter ConnexScript statements to manipulate the input data and define output. By default, the inputs have the variable names **in0**, **in1**, etc. Use these names to refer to the inputs in Script Editor. Outputs should be defined with the variable names **out0**, **out1**, etc.

- Choose **Apply Changes** from the **File** menu or click 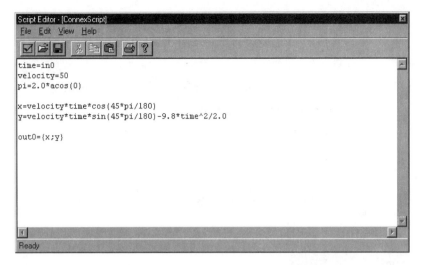.

- Choose **Close and Return** from the **File** menu or press [**Esc**].

Tip   Clicking ☑ runs the script so that you can see any errors while the Script Editor window is open.

For detailed information on ConnexScript syntax and built-in functions, see the section "Using ConnexScript" in Chapter 5. To edit the ConnexScript component, double-click it to activate it and make the necessary changes in the Script Editor.

Note   To use variable names other than **in0**, **in1**, etc. and **out0**, **out1**, etc., click the component with the right mouse button and choose **Properties** from the pop-up menu. Use the Input Variables page to change the input names. Use the Output Variables page to change the Output names.

Importing and exporting text in the ConnexScript component

You can import text from other files to the Script Editor and export text from the Script Editor to other files. The source file types recognized include ConnexScript and ASCII text.

To import the contents of another file into the Script Editor:

■ Position the cursor at the line where you want to import code.

■ Choose **Import** from the **File** menu, and browse to locate the file you want to import.

■ Click "Open."

To export the contents of the Script Editor to another file:

■ Choose **Export** from the **File** menu, and specify the path and filename of the target file.

■ Select the desired file type.

■ Click "Save."

The entire contents of the Script Editor window is exported to the target file.

Components for controlling data flow

When you connect two MathConnex components and run the system, the data flows from the output port of one component along the connecting wire to the input port of the next component. In some cases, however, you may want to halt the flow of data along the wire or control exactly which data values are passed through.

■ You can use the Stop/Pause component to stop a running system.

■ Using the Wire Breaker component you can quickly prevent or allow data to flow through a wire.

■ The Conditional component lets you send certain data values depending on whether a conditional statement is true or false.

■ The Initialize component lets you send data from the first input port of a component during the first run and from the second input port for subsequent runs.

Conditional

Using the Conditional component you can send either one set of data as output or another set depending on whether a conditional statement is true or false.

To insert the Conditional component into your Worksheet:

■ Drag the icon to the Worksheet. The Conditional component appears in your Worksheet.

■ Click the component with the right mouse button and choose **Properties** from the component's pop-up menu.

■ Click the Conditional tab, shown below.

■ In the "If" section, enter a single-line conditional expression using a ConnexScript statement as described in the section "Using ConnexScript" in Chapter 5.

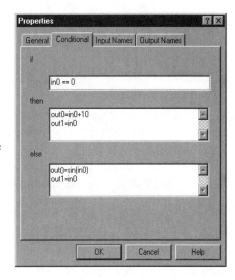

Some valid conditional statements include:

in0 < in1 *in0* is less than *in1*)

in0 < in1 & (in0!= 0 *in0* is less than *in1* AND *in0* is not equal to 0)

in0 = 10 *in0* is defined as 10)

in0 = = 0 (*in1* is equal to 0)

■ In the "Then" section, enter any number of ConnexScript statements to determine what the component outputs when the conditional statement is true. Use **in0**, **in1**, etc. and **out0**, **out1**, etc. to refer to the inputs and outputs, respectively.

■ In the "Else" section, enter any number of ConnexScript statements determining what the component outputs when the conditional statement is false. Use **in0**, **in1**, etc. and **out0**, **out1**, etc. to refer to the inputs and outputs respectively.

Note   The component defaults to having two input ports and two output ports, but you can add or remove any by using the appropriate commands on the component's pop-up menu.

An example of a system using the Conditional component is shown in Figure 4-8.

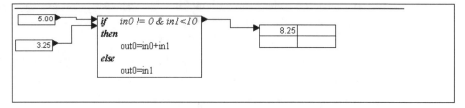

Figure 4-8: The Conditional component sends output based on whether the If" statement is true.

Note   You can use the Input Variables and the Output Variables tabs in the Properties dialog to specify different names for the inputs and outputs. For example, in Figure 4-9, the second output in the Conditional component is named **stop** rather than **out1**.

When a system containing the Conditional component runs, the Conditional component is triggered when it receives valid inputs. When it's triggered, it determines the output and sends it through the output port. If one of the outputs does not get defined when the component is triggered, no output is sent through its corresponding output port.

Tip   If you don't want any data to be sent when a statement is true or false, leave the "Then" or "Else" sections blank. If there are no statements in the "Else" section, that section does not appear when you look at the Conditional component in a system.

Initialize

Each time you run a system, a component usually takes input from all of its input ports. The Initialize component, however, takes input from one input port the first time you run the system and from another input port during subsequent runs. This is useful for iteration where an initial condition is set and then future values are passed back through the system.

To insert the Initialize component onto a Worksheet:

■   Drag the icon from the Component Palettes onto the Worksheet. The Initialize component appears in the Worksheet.

The Initialize component has two input ports. The component takes input from its top input port the first time data flows into the component. Each subsequent time, input is taken from the lower input port. The component's appearance changes to indicate when it is getting data from the top or bottom input port.

■   Connect the output ports of some component(s) to the top and bottom input ports of the Initialize component.

When you run the system for the first time, data flows into the Initialize component through the upper input port and back out. When the data flows into the component any other time, it flows in through the lower input port and back out.

Note   The Initialize component doesn't change the input in any way. It simply directs the input back into the system.

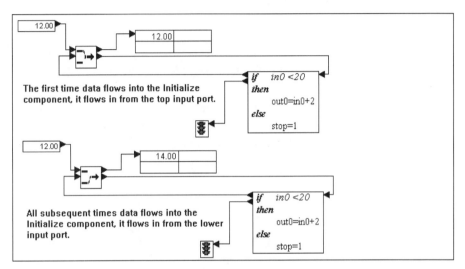

The first time data flows into the Initialize component, it flows in from the top input port.

```
if   in0 <20
then
        out0=in0+2
else
        stop=1
```

All subsequent times data flows into the Initialize component, it flows in from the lower input port.

```
if   in0 <20
then
        out0=in0+2
else
        stop=1
```

Figure 4-9: Using the Initialize component to specify a system's initial value.

Stop/Pause

To stop or pause a running system, you can always press the ⬛ button or the ⏸ button in the MathConnex toolbar or choose **Stop** or **Pause** from the **Run** menu. However, to avoid pressing these buttons every time you want to stop or pause a system, you can insert the Stop/Pause component into a system. This component stops or pauses a running a system when it receives data on its input wire.

To insert the Stop/Pause component:

- Drag the 🚦 icon from the Component Palettes onto the Worksheet. The Stop/Pause component appears.

- Connect the output port from a component to the input port of the Stop/ Pause component.

By default, when you run a system containing the Stop/Pause component, the system stops when a value is passed into it. To make the Stop/Pause component pause instead:

- Click the component with the right mouse button.

Components for controlling data flow   75

- Choose **Pause on Input** from the pop-up menu.

To make the Stop/Pause component beep when a data value goes into it:

- Click the component with the right mouse button.

- Choose **Beep When Active** from pop-up menu.

If you connect the Conditional component to the Stop/Pause component, you can force the system to stop or pause under certain conditions. In Figure 4-9, for example, the Stop/Pause component becomes active when a value exceeds 20.

Wire Breaker

As shown in Figure 4-10, using the Wire Breaker component you can easily alternate between allowing data to flow through a wire and preventing data from flowing through a wire.

To insert the Wire Breaker component:

- Drag the icon from the Component Palettes onto the Worksheet. The Wire Breaker component appears with one input port and one output port.

- Connect the output port from a component to the input port of the Wire Breaker component.

- Connect the output port from the Wire Breaker to the Input port of the next component in the system.

By default, the Wire Breaker component allows data to flow through it when you run the system. To prevent data from flowing:

- Click the component with the right mouse button.

- Choose **Disconnect the Wire** from the pop-up menu.

Tip   The Wire Breaker component is useful when part of a system takes a long time to calculate and you want to avoid passing data into it but want to keep the entire system connected.

To allow data to flow again:

- Click the component with the right mouse button.

- Choose **Connect the Wire** from the pop-up menu.

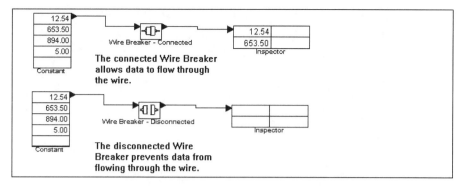

Figure 4-10: The Wire Breaker component allows you to selectively run parts of the system.

Note The Wire Breaker component, when connected, doesn't change the input in any way.

Other components

Many of the basic components are designed for manipulating data in a specified way. The Text component and the Scripted Object component are slightly different. The Text component does not manipulate data; it is simply an OLE object you can insert into a Worksheet to annotate it. The behavior of the Scripted Object component depends on how you script it.

Text

The Text component allows you to

■ Enter text anywhere above, below, or beside the components in the Worksheet.

■ Set the font, style, and size of the text.

Entering text

To place text on a Worksheet:

■ Drag the ▣ icon from the Component Palettes onto the Worksheet. You'll see the Text component window.

■ Begin typing text directly into the window.

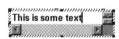

You can type beyond the length of the text box, but MathConnex displays only as much text as allowed by the width of the text box. If you want to display more text:

- Double-click the Text component to activate it.

- Move the cursor to the right or bottom handle until it changes to a double-headed arrow.

- Hold the mouse button down and drag outwards.

Changing the font and setting tabs

To change the font of the text in a Text component:

- Double-click the Text component to activate it.

- Choose **Set Fonts** from the **View** Menu.

- Select the font, style, and size of your text.

- Click "OK."

Note   The font settings are saved for each text component separately. You can have several Text components in your Worksheet and set the fonts differently for each.

To set the tab stops to a certain number of spaces:

- Double-click the Text component to activate it.

- Choose **Set Tab Stops** from the **View** Menu.

- Enter the number of spaces the [**Tab**] key should insert in the Text component.

- Click "OK."

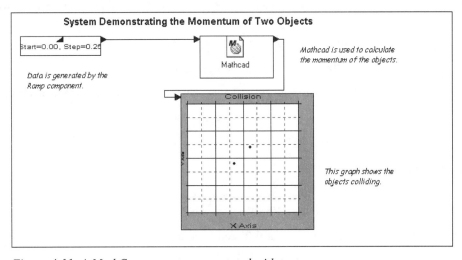

Figure 4-11: A MathConnex system annotated with text.

Editing the text in a text component

To cut, copy, paste, and delete text:

■ Double-click the Text component to activate it.

■ Drag-select text in the Text component.

■ Choose the appropriate option from the **Edit** menu.

Tip The **Edit** menu also gives you access to the **Find** and **Replace** commands for finding and replacing words in a Text component and automatically wrapping the text.

Scripted Object

You use the Scripted Object component to write a custom *script* (or program) for an OLE object so that it accepts input and sends output just like other built-in components.

To insert a Scripted Object component:

■ Drag the icon from the Component Palettes onto the Worksheet to launch the Scripting Wizard.

See Chapter 5, "Advanced Topics," for more information.

Chapter 5
Advanced Topics

This chapter introduces topics to help you get more out of MathConnex and to extend its functionality.

MathConnex run model

How components are triggered in MathConnex systems; parallel processing; feedback.

Scripted Object component

How to insert and configure a custom Scripted Object component to extend the functionality of MathConnex.

Using ConnexScript

Syntax, functions, and operators for use in the ConnexScript and Conditional components.

MathConnex run model

Chapter 3 introduced running, pausing, stopping, and single-stepping through a Math-Connex system. This section provides additional information about how MathConnex triggers the components of systems.

Filters, sinks, and sources

MathConnex is a visual tool that provides a data flow programming environment. MathConnex components in this environment fall into three functional categories:

- *Sources*, which introduce data into systems. Sources include the Input, File Read, and Ramp components.

- *Filters*, which take one or more data inputs and pass along one or more data outputs, usually with computational steps in between. Examples of filters are the Mathcad, S-PLUS Script, Excel, ConnexScript, and MATLAB computational components.

- *Sinks*, which receive data inputs and do not pass them further in a system, although they may process the data. The Stop/Pause component is the only true sink, although any component that is configured to have only input ports behaves as a sink.

Filters and sinks are triggered to run whenever they have received *all* of their input values on their input port(s). Sources, on the other hand, have one of two options:

- They may generate output once per system execution.

- They may generate output "continuously," i.e., as long as the system is running and all outputs are clear. An output is considered "clear" when the component on the other end of a wire has retrieved the last value from the wire.

Each source component has a **Continuous Output** command on its pop-up menu that controls which output behavior it will have. Select **Continuous Output** so that it is checked to make a component generate output continuously.

Note   When they are configured to have *only* output ports, the Mathcad, S-PLUS Script, Excel, ConnexScript, and MATLAB components behave as source components, and show the **Continuous Output** option on their pop-up menus.

When you run a system containing the Stop/Pause component, the system stops or pauses automatically when a value is passed into this component. If you run a system that does not contain this component, the system runs continuously until you pause or stop it using the ▯▯ or ▮ Toolbar button or the corresponding command on the **Run** menu.

Parallel processing and execution steps

In MathConnex, parallel paths of execution can be accomplished in two ways:

■ By placing two or more unconnected systems on the Worksheet.

■ By branching along multiple paths by using multiple output wires from a single component. These wires may take different paths through the system.

When you run your system(s), all components—even those in unconnected systems—that are able to begin running at a particular time constitute a *time step* in execution. The slowest component that is able to run within a time step determines when the next time step begins. The overall speed of the system is the sum of the time steps.

You can always see the exact order of execution in your system(s) by selecting **Highlight Components** from the **Run** menu and then repeatedly choosing **Step** from the **Run** menu.

The **Single Step Mode** command on the **Run** menu allows you to control how you step through the parallel parts of the system. If you check **Single Step Mode** on the **Run** menu, MathConnex alternates through the steps in each system one at a time as each component is ready; otherwise, MathConnex moves through all systems concurrently as the next set of components becomes ready.

Feedback

Although not explicitly designed as a simulation environment, MathConnex can be applied to feedback problems that arise in engineering, physical, and life sciences. The critical component for simulating feedback is the Initialize component, which you insert

into the Worksheet by dragging the ▨ button from the Component Palettes.

Tip If you installed MathConnex with Mathcad 8 Professional, several of the sample MathConnex projects in the SAMPLES folder use the Initialize component.

The Initialize component takes input from the upper input port the first time you run the system and from the lower input port during subsequent runs. Typically you pass *initial conditions* for a system through the first input port of the Initialize component, and you then feed values computed further down in the system back into the second input port to begin a new cycle (*feedback loop*) of computation. Unless you are designing a system to run continuously, you must define some termination condition in your system, usually with a Conditional component, to stop the feedback loop.

Note If you plan to feed several values back through a system, you usually need to pass a *vector* of values through the Initialize component.

Scripted Object component

MathConnex has specific components for managing interapplication data flow with Mathcad, S-PLUS, Axum, Excel, and MATLAB. However, you can exchange data between MathConnex components and any object that supports OLE 2 Automation, even if MathConnex does not have a specific component to do so. You use the Scripted Object component to write a custom *script* (or program) for an object so that it:

- Accepts values from MathConnex components that are wired to its input port(s).

- Activates the server application or control to manipulate the data when the Math-Connex system is running.

- Sends values to MathConnex components wired to its output port(s).

To create a Scripted Object component, you must:

- Be proficient in a supported scripting language, such as Microsoft VBScript or JScript, that is installed on your system.

- Understand the way the OLE server, OLE control, or ActiveX control that you wish to script has implemented OLE Automation.

- Have the server or control available on your system.

More on scripting languages

Before you insert a Scripted Object component into the MathConnex Worksheet, you need to have a supported scripting language installed on your system. As this *User's Guide* goes to press, the following two scripting languages are supported: Microsoft VBScript (Visual Basic Scripting Edition) and Microsoft JScript (an implementation of JavaScript). Both of these scripting languages are included with Microsoft Internet Explorer, which can be installed from the Mathcad installation media. These scripting languages can also be downloaded at no charge from Microsoft, Inc. at:

http://www.microsoft.com/scripting

Note   VBScript is a strict *subset* of the Visual Basic for Applications language used in Microsoft Excel, Project, Access, and the Visual Basic development system. VBScript is designed to be a lightweight interpreted language, so it does not use strict types (only Variants). Also, because VBScript is intended to be a safe subset of the language, it does not include file input/output or direct access to the underlying operating system. JScript is a fast, portable, lightweight interpreter for use in applications that use ActiveX controls, OLE automation servers, and Java applets. JScript is directly comparable to VBScript (not Java). Like VBScript, JScript is a pure interpreter that processes source code rather than producing stand-alone applets. The syntax and techniques used in the scripting language you choose are beyond the scope of this *User's Guide*.

Inserting a Scripted Object component

To insert a Scripted Object component into the MathConnex Worksheet:

■ Drag the ![icon] icon from the Component Palettes onto the Worksheet, or choose **Scripted Object** from the **Insert** menu, to launch the Scripting Wizard.

This launches the Scripting Wizard. First specify the OLE server, OLE control, or ActiveX control from which you want to create a Scripted Object. The Object to Script scrolling list shows available objects on your system. Choose an object that supports the OLE2 Automation interface.

Note   The fact that an object appears on the Object to Script scrolling list does not necessarily indicate that it supports the OLE 2 Automation interface to work as a Scripted Object in MathConnex. You'll need to consult the documentation for any OLE server, OLE control, or ActiveX control you script in MathConnex.

You must specify:

■ Whether the component is a new file or whether you will insert an existing file.

■ Whether you will see the actual file or an icon in your MathConnex worksheet.

In the remaining pages of the Wizard you specify: the scripting language you are using, the type of object you want to script, the name of the object, and the number of inputs and outputs the object will accept and provide.

Properties of the component

Like other OLE objects you insert into the Worksheet, a Scripted Object component has the following properties:

■ You select the object in the Worksheet by clicking it once. Move, cut, copy, and delete the selected object like any other MathConnex component.

■ Double-click the object to activate it or to resize it. Unless you inserted an icon, you'll see the object activate in-place for editing, and the menus and toolbars will change to those of the other application. Click outside the object to resume working in MathConnex.

Unlike other OLE objects you insert into the Worksheet, however, a Scripted Object component displays input and output ports and can pass data in a MathConnex system:

■ Click once with the right mouse button to see a pop-up menu for the component. You access a properties page, configure the run options, and add and remove input and output ports by choosing commands from the pop-up menu.

■ Connect the component to other MathConnex components in the usual way, by drawing a wire from another component's output port to an input port or from an output port to another component's input port.

Object model

The Scripted Object component has the following predefined objects, properties, and methods that enable you to configure it to work as a MathConnex component.

Collections

■ **Inputs** and **Outputs** are predefined *collections* of DataValue objects (see below) containing the Scriptable Object's inputs and the outputs, respectively.

■ The **Count** property can be used to query the total number of elements in the collection. For example, **Outputs.Count** returns the number of output variables.

■ The **Item** method is used to specify an individual element in the collection. To refer to a particular input or output, use the notation **Inputs.Item(*n*)** or **Outputs.Item(*n*)**, where *n* is the index of the input or output. The index *n* always starts from 0. Since **Item** is the default method, languages such as VBScript and JScript let you drop the method name to imply the default method. For example, **Inputs(0)** is equivalent to **Inputs.Item(0)** and references the first input.

DataValue objects

■ The **Value** property accesses a DataValue's real part. For example, in VBScript or JScript **Inputs(0).Value** returns the real part of the first input.

■ The **IValue** property accesses a DataValue's imaginary part. For example, in VBScript or JScript **Outputs(1).IValue** returns the imaginary part of the second output. If there is no imaginary part, the **IValue** portion returns "NIL."

■ The **IsComplex** property returns "TRUE" if a DataValue has a valid imaginary part; this property returns "FALSE" otherwise. For example, the expression **(inputs(0).IsComplex)** returns "FALSE" if the first input has only a real part.

■ The **Rows** and **Cols** properties yield the number of rows and columns.

Global methods

■ The **alert** function takes a single string parameter that is presented to the user as a standard modal Windows message box with an "OK" button.

■ The **errmsg** function takes a string parameter that appears as an error message from within the script and causes the script to stop execution. A second, optional parameter is a string used to display the source of the error.

Note   In JScript, the names of functions, methods, objects, and properties are case sensitive, while in VBScript they are not.

Scripting the object

To start scripting an inserted Scripted Object component:

■ Click once on the component with the right mouse button to see the pop-up menu.

■ Choose **Edit Script** from the pop-up menu.

You'll see a new window called the Script Editor containing three subroutine stubs in which you insert your own scripting code. Figure 5-1 shows an example of the VBScript shell you'd see for a new scripted object called **MyScriptedObj**.

The script you write usually contains at a minimum the following three subroutines:

■ A *starting* routine, called once when execution of the system begins. This is a good place to initialize variables, open files for reading and writing, etc.

■ An *execution* routine, called every time the component receives or outputs data values. By default it takes as arguments the collections **Inputs** and **Outputs**.

■ A *stopping* routine, called once when execution of the system stops.

What you will include in these subroutines is determined largely by the properties of the OLE object you are scripting; consult the documentation for the server or control.

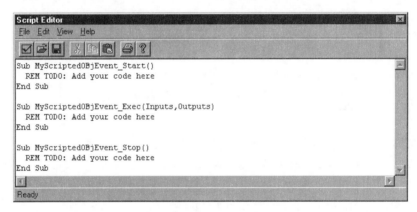

Figure 5-1: The Script Editor window shows the VBScript shell for an object named **MyScriptedObj**. *You write the code to configure the object.*

To resume working in MathConnex when you have finished writing your script, choose **Close and Return** from the Script Editor's **File** menu, or press [**Esc**].

Tip   If you installed MathConnex with Mathcad 8 Professional, see the SAMPLES folder in the location where you installed Mathcad and MathConnex for examples of Scripted Object components with working scripts. Bear in mind that to run these sample projects with Scripted Object components, you will need to install any applications or controls that were used to create those components.

Using ConnexScript

ConnexScript is a lightweight mathematical programming language you use in the ConnexScript and Conditional components of MathConnex. It provides basic scientific calculator functionality and is particularly useful for computational flow control in cases where you don't need the full functionality of the Mathcad, S-PLUS Script, Excel, or MATLAB component.

ConnexScript has a familiar mathematical syntax similar to that in popular matrix language products. In addition, many mathematical operators, such as matrix multiplication and division, are built into the language, as are basic and user-defined mathematical functions.

Data types

ConnexScript supports real and complex data.

Real numbers

ConnexScript uses double-precision, IEEE format floating point numbers. E-format notation is supported.

Examples
```
314          3.14          5.78e14
```

Complex numbers

Complex numbers consist of:

■ a real part, which is a real number.

■ an imaginary part, which is stored as a real number but is equivalent to a real number multiplied by the square root of -1.

To facilitate entering complex numbers, ConnexScript supports both the i and j notation appended to the end of numerical constants to indicate an imaginary number.

Examples
```
5.78i               0.5e10i               4.0 + 8.7j
```

Infinite and Not-a-Number

ConnexScript has built-in support for Infinite (**Inf**) and Not-a-Number (**NaN**) values, which can often result from errors in calculations. Infinite and Not-a-Number values can also be assigned to variables directly, using the pre-defined variables **Inf** and **NaN**, as well as their capitalized and uncapitalized permutations (**inf**, **Nan**, etc.).

Examples
```
x = Inf          y = NaN
```

Operators

Operator	Description
=	assignment
+	addition
–	subtraction
*	multiplication
/	division
^	power
.*	elementwise matrix multiplication
./	elementwise matrix division
.^	elementwise matrix power
~	logical (Boolean) NOT
xor	logical (Boolean) XOR
!=	not equal to
>=	greater than or equal to
<=	less than or equal to
&	logical (Boolean) AND
|	logical (Boolean) OR
==	equal to
>	greater than
<	less than

Note Addition, subtraction, multiplication, division, and power can take either scalar or array arguments.

Functions

In general, ConnexScript built-in functions take either real or complex arguments. User-defined functions are discussed on page 97. Function names are case sensitive.

Basic math functions

Function	Description
abs	returns absolute value
ceil	rounds up to next integer
exp	exponential
floor	rounds down to previous integer
log10	computes base 10 logarithm
log2	computes base 2 logarithm
ln	natural logarithm
max	returns maximum value of variable
min	returns minimum value of variable
mod	returns the remainder after the first argument is divided by the second.
nelem	returns the number of elements in a variable
round	rounds a value to the closest integer
sign	returns the sign of the input variable
sqrt	returns square root of input variable
time	returns number of seconds since January 1, 1980
trunc	drops the decimal portion of a value

Complex math functions

Function	Description
conj	returns complex conjugate
im	returns imaginary part of a number
re	returns real part of input variable

Trigonometric functions

Function	Description
cos	cosine
sin	sine
tan	tangent
sec	secant
csc	cosecant
cot	cotangent
pi	returns the value of pi
acsc	arc/inverse cosecant
acos	arc/inverse cosine
acot	arc/inverse cotangent
asec	arc/inverse secant
asin	arc/inverse sine
atan	arc/inverse tangent

Hyperbolic trigonometric functions

Function	Description
cosh	hyperbolic cosine
coth	hyperbolic tangent
csch	hyperbolic cosecant
sech	hyperbolic secant
sinh	hyperbolic sine
tanh	hyperbolic tangent
acsch	arc/inverse hyperbolic cosecant
acosh	arc/inverse hyperbolic cosine
acoth	arc/inverse hyperbolic cotangent
asech	arc/inverse hyperbolic secant
asinh	arc/inverse hyperbolic sine
atanh	arc/inverse hyperbolic tangent

Matrix and special functions

Function	Description
cols	returns number of columns in a matrix
rows	returns number of rows in a matrix
det	returns determinant of a matrix
gamma	returns gamma function

Miscellaneous functions

Function	Description
delete	deletes a variable from current program level
error	returns user-defined message text when an error is encountered

Reserved words

The following words cannot be used as variable or function names:

break	elseif	if	NaN	return
cols	end	in	nelem	rows
complex	error	Inf	new	static
delete	for	list	real	until
else	function	load	repeat	while
				xor

Variables

Variables in ConnexScript:

- must begin with an alphabetical character

- may contain a combination of letters and numbers, including an underscore character (_)

- may not be the same as one of the ConnexScript reserved words

- may not contain special characters that are used as ConnexScript operators

- may not contain an embedded space

- are case sensitive

Examples

`this_is_my_variable`	`t1`
`x_5`	`R2D2`

Note In a ConnexScript or Conditional component, you use the variable names **in0**, **in1**, etc. by default for inputs and the variable names **out0**, **out1**, etc. for outputs.

Creating vectors and matrices

ConnexScript supports creation of vectors and matrices in two ways:

- static array notation

- colon vector notation

Static array notation

In a static array declaration:

- curly braces (**{** and **}**) are used to denote the beginning and end of the static declaration

- the comma (**,**) is used to separate values along the same row

- the semicolon (**;**) is used to separate the next row

```
{ expr, expr ; expr, expr }
```

For example, to create a row vector using static array notation, you would type:

```
x = { 1, 2, 3 }
```

To create a 2 by 3 matrix using static array notation you would type:

```
x = { 1, 2, 3; 4, 5, 6 }
```

Note   The semicolon begins the second row. When multiple rows are declared, the lengths of the vectors representing each row must be equal.

Example 1
```
{ 1, x, (y*z) ; z, 2.89, 4 }
```   *// semicolon indicates new row*

Example 2
```
x = { 1, 2, 3, 4 }
```        *// 1-by-4 vector*

```
A = { 1, 2, 3; 4, 5, 6 }
```        *// 2-by-3 matrix*

Colon vector notation

In a colon vector declaration, start, end, and optional step values are used to automatically generate a range of values for a vector, where the colon (:) is used to separate the expressions.

```
start_expr : step_expr : end_expr
```

For example, to create a vector spanning the values for 1 to 100, in increments of 2, you would type

```
x = 1:2:100
```

When the step value is omitted, ConnexScript defaults to a step value of 1, or, when the start value is greater than the end value, a step value of –1.

Examples
```
y = 1:10
```     *// default step 1*
```
y = 10:1
```     *// automatically step -1*
```
a = 1:5:1000
```      *//1 to 1000 step 5*

Expressions

A ConnexScript expression is some combination of variables, constants, operators, and functions that indicates the computation of a value.

Constant expressions

Constant expressions contain only constant values:

```
7                         7 + 8 * 19 / 3.3
```

Variable expressions

Variable expressions contain simple variables or simple variables and operators:

```
x                    x + 8              x / y * 8
```

Indexed variable expressions

Indexed variable expressions contain vectors or array variables which are to be indexed:

```
x = y[5]            A[3] = B[5;3] * x
```

Note   ConnexScript uses zero-based indexing, so 0 is the first element, 1 is the second element, etc.

Function call expressions

Function call expressions contain function invocations: either built-in functions or user-defined functions, as in this example:

```
y = sin(x)
```

Numerical Expressions

Numerical expressions contain a numerical operator:

expr + *expr*	scalar or matrix addition
expr - *expr*	scalar or matrix subtraction
expr * *expr*	scalar or matrix multiplication
expr .* *expr*	elementwise matrix multiplication
expr ^ *expr*	scalar or matrix power
expr .^ *expr*	elementwise matrix power
expr / *expr*	scalar division or matrix right division
expr ./ *expr*	elementwise matrix division

Boolean conditional expressions

Boolean conditional expressions contain a Boolean logical or relational operator:

~ *expr*	logical NOT
expr xor *expr*	logical exclusive-OR
expr | *expr*	logical OR
expr & *expr*	logical AND
expr == *expr*	equality comparison
expr != *expr*	inequality comparison
expr < *expr*	less than comparison
expr <= *expr*	less than or equal to comparison
expr > *expr*	greater than comparison
expr >= *expr*	greater than or equal to comparison

Comments

ConnexScript supports both in-line and multiple-line comments.

In-line comments

Double forward slashes (//) begin code comments that go to the end of the line.

Example
```
x = A[1,2;0]        // take first element from 2nd and 3rd row
```

The text typed following the **//** (displayed here in italics) is ignored.

Multiple-line comments

A forward slash followed by an asterisk (**/***) begins a multiple-line comment, and an asterisk followed by a forward slash (***/**) ends a multiple-line comment. The text inside the **/*** and ***/** is ignored.

Statements

Multiple statements

ConnexScript supports multiple statements on a line. The statements must be separated by a semicolon (**;**).

```
statement ; statement
```

Examples
```
x = y + 5; z = x^2

x = 0; for i in 0:5; x = x + i; end
```

Line continuation

An underscore (_) followed by a carriage return indicates continuation of a line of code.

Example
```
A = { 1, 2, 3; _
      4, 5, 6; _
      7, 8, 9 }      // 3-by-3 matrix
```

Function call statements

ConnexScript functions have the following calling sequence:

```
result = funcname ( argument1,  argument2,  ... )
```

where **result** is the returned value of the function stated in **funcname**; **argument1**, **argument2**, etc., are any required parameters; and the comma is required between arguments (parameters).

Example
```
y = sin( x )        // call a built-in function
```

If statement

The ConnexScript **if** statement is used with the **elseif** and **else** statements for conditional branching.

```
if boolean_expr
     statement1
     statement2
     ...
elseif boolean_expr
```

```
        statement3
        ...
else
        statement4
        ...
end
```

In an **if** statement, when the ***boolean_expr*** following the **if** evaluates to "true" (nonzero), the statements within the **if** block are executed. Otherwise, execution skips over the if block to the **elseif** condition (if present) or directly to the **else** block (if present). The **elseif** block and the **else** block are optional.

If the **elseif** block is present, the statement following the **elseif** is executed whenever the **if** *boolean_expr* evaluates to "false" (zero) and the **elseif** ***boolean_expr*** evaluates to "true" (nonzero). You may have more than one **elseif** block.

If the **else** block is present, the statement following the else is executed whenever the preceding if and elseif expressions (if present) evaluate to "false" (zero).

Example
```
if( x > y & x != 0 )
       z = y / x
       q = log(2^z)
elseif( y >= x & y != 0 )
       z = x / y
       q = 2^z
else
       z = 0
       q = 1
end
```

For statement

The **for** statement is an iterative, or looping, statement.

```
for identifier in expr
       statement1
       statement2
       ...
end
```

In a **for** statement, a scalar value (***identifier***) is iterated over a range of values given in the expression (***expr***). Each successive iteration updates the loop value to the next value in the expression. For example, **for i in 1:10** iterates the value **i** over the range 1–10, as given by the colon vector expression **1:10**.

Typically, the expression is a colon vector of the form **1:10**, or the number of elements in columns or rows of a matrix, such as **0:(rows(A) - 1)**.

As in a Mathcad for loop, the start and end range need not be sequential. For example, if **x** is a vector containing the elements **{1, 3, 8, 23, 47}**, we can use **x** as a source of indices into a matrix **A** as follows:

```
y = 0
for i in x
      y = y + A[i]
end
```

Tip   The **break** statement can be inserted inside of a loop to terminate the loop prematurely.

While statement

The **while** statement is a conditional looping statement that is executed repeatedly while a condition remains true.

```
while expr
      statement1
      statement2
      ...
end
```

In a **while** statement, when the condition expression (**expr**) following the **while** evaluates to "true" (nonzero), the statements inside the while block are executed. After the statements contained within the **while–end** are executed, program control returns to the top of the loop. The process repeats until the condition expression evaluates to "false" (zero).

Example
```
i = 0
while( i < 100 )                    // using while loop
      A[i] = A[i] * 4
      i = i + 1
end
```

Tip   The **break** statement can be inserted inside of a loop to terminate the loop prematurely.

User-defined functions

When one of the ConnexScript built-in functions does not satisfy your requirements, you can write a new function using the function declaration. You may define a function anywhere in your ConnexScript script. The function declaration has the form:

```
function funcname ( paramdef1, paramdef2, ... )
      statement1
      statement2
      ...
      return
end
```

where each **paramdef** is the name of a variable passed into the function. All variables are passed by reference. The **return** statement is optional, and can be placed anywhere inside the function in order to "return" from the function prematurely or due to some programmatic condition. Upon reaching the final end statement, the function automatically returns the value of the variable **funcname**, which you need to assign somewhere in the body of your program.

Return value

ConnexScript functions return their value by assignment to a variable of the same name as the function. The return statement does not take any additional arguments. For example, to return a value from the function **myfunc**, you would simply assign a value to the variable named **myfunc** inside the function body, as with the statement **myfunc = x + y**. By default, functions have a return value of 0.0. User-defined functions may call themselves recursively.

Environment

The ConnexScript component can automatically load ConnexScript files with the .MXS extension that are located in the MXSLIB folder. When a function called in a Connex-Script script is not found by its name as a built-in function or as a user-defined function in the script and a .MXS file with the same name as the function exists in the MXSLIB folder, the .MXS file is loaded.

Reusable ConnexScript commands can be placed in a separate file and then "included" in a ConnexScript component via the **load** command:

```
load "drive:\folder\filename"
```

The path to the file to be loaded must be specified and enclosed in double quotes. Relative paths can be specified. Typically, the **load** command is used to access sets of constant values or common functions from multiple ConnexScript components.

Tip   ConnexScript files typically have the .MXS extension, but any text file can be loaded.

Index

3D Graph component 54
3D graphs 54, 58, 60
    rotating 57
    spinning 57
    zooming 57
accumulating data 51
ActiveX control 84
Add Component command 18
adding breakpoints 33
adding input ports 25, 40
adding output ports 25, 40
Axum component 58
bar plots (3D) 56
breakpoints
    adding 33
    removing 34
calculations 62, 66, 69–70
Collapse command 13
collapsed system 8
complex threshold
    in the Input component 45
    in the Inspector component 51
Component Palettes 10
components
    3D Graph component 54
    activating 28
    adding and deleting 18
    adding and removing ports 25
    Axum component 58
    Component Palettes 10
    Conditional component 72
    connecting 30
    ConnexScript component 70
    copying 26
    cutting 26
    deleting 26
    disconnecting 30
    displayed as icons 35, 41
    displayed as objects 36
    drag and drop 10
    enlarging or shrinking 24
    Excel component 66
    File Read/Write component 46
    flipping port direction of 25
    Global Variable component 48
    Graph component 52
    highlighting 32

    Initialize component 74
    Input component 43
    Inspector component 49
    labeling 37
    levels 11
    Mathcad component 62
    MATLAB component 69
    moving 23–24
    overview 20, 40
    pasting 26
    placing on the Worksheet 21, 40
    properties of 27, 42
    Ramp component 47
    resizing 24
    Scripted Object component 79
    S-PLUS Graph component 60
    S-PLUS Script component 64
    Stop/Pause component 75
    Text component 77
    Wire Breaker component 76
Conditional component 72
connecting components
    using the Wire Breaker component 76
    with wires 30
ConnexScript component 70
    environment 97
    importing and exporting scripts 71
    including functions 97
ConnexScript language
    in Conditional component 72
    in ConnexScript component 70
    reference 88
context menu
    See pop-up menu
Continuous Output 82
contour plots 55
copying components 26
cutting components 26
data
    accumulating 51
    entering into a table 43
    exporting 51
    generating 47
    graphing 52, 54, 58
    importing 44
    manipulating 62, 66, 69–70
    pasting from the Clipboard 44
    reading in 46
    viewing 34, 49
    writing out 46
deleting cells in Input component 45

disconnecting components 30
    using the Wire Breaker component 76
displayed precision
    in the Input component 45
    in the Inspector component 51
displaying components as icons 35
displaying components as objects 36
double-clicking components 28
drag and drop 14
Edit Object command 35
else statement 72
emailing a project 7
Excel component 66
Expand command 13
exponential threshold
    in the Input component 45
    in the Inspector component 51
feedback 83
File Read/Write component 46
filters 82
flip port direction 25
generating values 47
Global Variable component 48
go back to higher level of Worksheet 8, 13
Graph component 52
graphing
    with 3D Graph component 54
    with Axum component 58
    with Graph component 52
graphs
    2D 52
    3D 54
    Axum 58
    S-PLUS 60
Help 4, 8
highlighting active components 32
if statement 72
importing data from a file 44
Initialize component 74
Input component 43
    display format 44
Insert Component command 41
Insert Object command 15
inspecting values on a wire 34, 49
Inspector component 49
IntelliMouse support 58
JavaScript 84
JScript 84
labeling a component 37
language, ConnexScript 88
locking a subsystem 13

magnifying glass 34
mail 7
MAPI 16
Mathcad component 62
MathConnex
    Component Palettes 10
    Explorer 16
    features 2
    installation 6
    menus 7
    modules 17
    overview 2
    projects 16
    run model 82
    running a system 31
    Status Bar 9
    Toolbar 7, 9
    Worksheet 11
    workspace 5
MathSoft World Wide Web site 4
MATLAB component 69
    importing and exporting scripts 70
memory 3
menus 7
    Edit 7
    File 7
    Help 8
    Insert 8
    Run 8
    View 7
Microsoft Internet Explorer 84
modules 15
    exporting and importing 17
Modules tab 17
moving components 23
MXSLIB folder 97
OLE
    automation 84
    control 84
    object, inserting into project 8, 14
    server 84
on-line Help 4, 8
parallel processing 83
parametric surface plots 55
pasting components 26
pausing a system 11, 33, 75
pop-up menu
    3D Graph component 54–55
    component 42
    Excel component 68
    Inspector component 50

Mathcad component 64
Scriptable Object component 87
S-PLUS Graph component 60
S-PLUS Script component 65
ports, adding and removing 25, 40
precision
    in the Input component 45
    in the Inspector component 51
printing a project 7, 15
project
    emailing 7
    inserting a Scripted Object 8
    inserting an OLE object 8
    new 7
    opening 7
    printing 7, 15
    saving 7
projects 15
Projects tab 16
properties 27
    of components 42
Ramp component 47
reading from a data file 46
removing breakpoints 34
removing input ports 25, 40
removing output ports 25, 40
rotating 3D graphs 57
run mode 9
run model, of MathConnex 82
run to a certain point 34
running a system 31, 34
sample projects 4
scatter plots (3D) 55
Scripted Object component 79, 84
    inserting into a project 8
    object model 86
scrollbars 28
show labels 37
show row/column labels
    in the Input component 45
    in the Inspector component 51
show trailing zeros
    in the Input component 45
    in the Inspector component 51
Single Step Mode command 83

sinks 82
sources 82
spinning 3D graphs 57
S-PLUS Graph component 60
S-PLUS Script component 64
    importing and exporting scripts 66
Status Bar 9
stepping through a system 32
Stop/Pause component 75
stopping a system 11, 31, 33, 75
stopping data flow 76
surface plots 55
system
    collapsing and expanding 13
    creating 11
    locking a subsystem 13
    running 31
Text component 14, 77
then statement 72
Toolbar 7, 9
unlocking a subsystem 13
VBScript 84
vector field plots 56
view as icon 35
view as object 36
Visual Basic Scripting Edition 84
Wire Breaker component 76
wires
    adding 30
    removing 30
Wizard
    for inserting a component 40
    for scripted object 85
Worksheet 11
    annotation 14
    collapsed system 8
    run mode 9
workspace 5
writing to a data file 46
zero threshold
    in the Input component 45
    in the Inspector component 51
zooming
    3D graphs 57
    Worksheet 13